A Warm and Welcome Place

HEART TO HEART WITH

JUNE STRONG

REVIEW AND HERALD® PUBLISHING ASSOCIATION
HAGERSTOWN, MD 21740

Copyright © 1993 by
Review and Herald® Publishing Association

The author assumes full responsibility for the accuracy of all facts and quotations as cited in this book.

Unless otherwise indicated all Scripture references are from the *Holy Bible, New International Version.* Copyright © 1973, 1978, 1984, International Bible Society. Used by permission of Zondervan Bible Publishers.

Texts credited to NKJV are from The New King James Version. Copyright © 1979, 1980, 1982, Thomas Nelson, Inc., Publishers.

This book was
Edited by Richard W. Coffen
Designed by Bill Kirstein
Cover design/illustration by Scott Snow
Typeset: 11.2/13.2 Palatino

PRINTED IN U.S.A.

98 97 96 95 94   10 9 8 7 6 5 4 3 2

R&H Cataloging Service
Strong, June (Kimball)
    A warm and welcome place.

    1. Christian life—Seventh-day Adventist
authors. 2. Devotional literature—Seventh-day
Adventist authors. I. Title.
        248.486

ISBN 0-8280-0730-6

For
Allison June Strong,
the newest bud on our
family tree

Also by June Strong

Journal of a Happy Woman
Mindy
My Little Journey
Project Sunlight
Song of Eve
Where Are We Running?

Contents

The Divine "Yes"

O ne of our little grandchildren is a blond boy just shoving his tiny shoulder against the gates of the terrible twos. "No" is his favorite word. Sometimes when I go to visit him, before I even utter a greeting he scowls and unfurls his flag of resistance. "No, no, no!"

But somewhere in the midst of all that negativism, he also learned to say "Yes." Well, not really yes, but his lisping equivalent—"Yeth." And when he utters it, it is filled with sweetness and light. He puts more expression into that little three-letter word than some people manage in an afternoon's conversation. He uses it shyly, as though the concept is something new and fragile—something puzzling, yet delightful, stumbled upon in the land of No.

"Are you ready for lunch, Eric?"

"Yeth." A little smile.

And "yeth" sounds like "If it's not too much trouble, Grandma" or "You're so sweet to ask me." A rainbow in the storm of "Nos."

Yes is, indeed, a magical word. I saw once on television an honest-to-goodness proposal of marriage. No fictional fantasy, but a real young man asking a real young woman for a life commitment. She'd been hoping for such a moment so long that when it came—and on TV, no less—astonishment left her momentarily speechless. Then, tears trickling down her cheeks and her eyes shining, she said, "Yes, yes, oh, yes!" I don't know how other onlookers reacted, but I felt like a Peeping Tom. This moment was far too personal to be sandwiched between detergent commercials and shared by the entire country. However, I never will forget her radiant face, nor her joyous acceptance.

"Yes, yes, oh, yes!" How that little word yes can change one's entire life, for better or for worse.

Ann Kiemel once wrote a wonderful book entitled *Yes!* in which she shared her struggle to submit to God in every area of her life.

But our scripture presents the flip side of the Christian's yes. It's *God's* yes to us. Paul vows that God's every promise is sure and possible through Christ. A yes from God has supernatural power behind it—divine, miraculous power. It accomplishes the impossible, makes sinners into saints, creates love where there is only emptiness, brings order out of chaos, and, if necessary, patiently waits for a break-through.

Ann Kiemel put it this way:

"YES

Because Jesus is the divine Yes.

Because He changes everything.

He is my highest fulfillment.

He made me whole . . .

Takes the bad and turns it to good.

He is my Song . . .

My Reason to live" (*Yes*, p. 12).

Is Jesus *your* song, *your* reason to live?

Choose a favorite hymn that exalts Him. Sing it as you drive to work or juggle the schedule of your busy household. He is the yes in our lives today, tomorrow, and forever. That's cause to celebrate.

For no matter how many promises God has made, they are "Yes" in Christ (2 Cor. 1:20).

My Forever Friend

Not long ago in an old scrapbook, I came across a large cartoon-type clipping from a newspaper. In it a bearded young man, obviously Jesus, leans against a lamppost on a busy city street. As they pass Him, one pedestrian remarks to another, "Hey, isn't that What's-His-Name?"

The drawing, with its haunting message, always startles me. Maybe "startles" isn't the right word. I guess it hurts me. Because the young Man leaning on the lamppost is my friend. He has made a tremendous investment in my future. He considered our relationship so valuable that He did not hesitate to take my place when I was faced with worse than death. One does not have many such friends.

He's a very low-key kind of person. Had the passerby and his flippant remark been real, Jesus would not have been offended. He doesn't seem to have any ego problems. He's totally at ease, and that makes me very comfortable with Him.

He has everything I need, and He would never consider withholding any portion of it from me. Yet He's taught me that I don't need very much. The simplicity of His life often shames the complexity of mine, though He says not a word.

He doesn't ever seem to hurry, compete, or worry. In fact, He seems to have only one concern, and that's for all those people streaming by on the city sidewalk. He has suggested, from time to time, that He wished I felt a compelling compassion for them also, for He is aware that He's lost any real meaning for most of them—and they need Him. More than they could ever know. He has this idea that maybe I could be a go-between because somehow I seem more real to most of them.

I've tried to convince one here and there that He is the key figure in our present situation, but most of them brush me aside impatiently. They're discussing important things, such as the stock market or how to deal with child abuse. Or less important things, like Maybelline's new mascara or what's playing at the Kennedy Center. I get easily discouraged. They're used to taking care of themselves. As long as their health and their money hold out, they don't really want to hear about their needs. They aren't sure they have any.

I've heard that my Friend is much more popular in Third World nations. Or in countries in which war has ravaged the land and its people. When you are cold and hungry and your loved ones are dead or dying, you begin to notice the young Man leaning against the lamppost.

But the successful people are all a little afraid of my friend. Afraid He's going to strip them of all life's shiny baubles. I'll admit I entertained some of those fears myself. But I really wanted what He had. I wanted that serenity that gives Him such poise, making Him move so easily among us, yet somehow so far above and beyond us. Cautiously I surrendered just one area of my life, then another, to Him. The bondage I feared never materialized. Instead there was a new freedom, like a long-lost heritage out of the far past. I'm still in the process. Sometimes—oh, shameful admission—I become like the people on the street, completely zeroed in on what's happening here and now.

But there is one strategic difference. You see, I told Him long ago that I wanted to be His friend forever. That I might often get off course, but, at whatever cost, I wanted Him to bring me back to His side. So sometimes when I'm lost in the crowd, my foolish mind numb to His love, I feel a hand upon my shoulder, and when I turn He smiles that gentle, tender smile which sets a candle burning in my heart. And then we walk together once again.

Just in case He's only What's-His-Name to you, I invite you to slow your pace and join us. No need for introductions. He already knows your name.

I am with you and will watch over you wherever you go (Gen. 28:15).

Jenny's Question

Waiting patiently for my attention, 7-year-old Jenny stood at my elbow as adult conversation ebbed and flowed around her. An urgency in her courteous restraint alerted my grandmotherly awareness.

"What is it, love?" I invited, putting an arm about her skinny blue-jeaned body.

"You know what, Grandma? There's no Santa Claus." Her eyes met mine warily. How would I respond to such a cataclysmic revelation?

She had spoken, happily and confidently, of the old holiday hero just days before, so I understood a traumatic disillusionment had taken place. I had the feeling she was hoping I'd heartily deny her pronouncement. But I'd never been much in favor of the Saint Nick spoof to begin with, and I certainly didn't intend to perpetuate it.

"No, there really isn't," I agreed, "but the legend is part of Christmas, like Rudolph, the red-nosed reindeer. You don't have to throw him out completely."

She hardly heard me. "And there's no such thing as monsters . . . or ET." I could see she and her mother had had an in-depth discussion on fantasy figures. "Or ghosts or witches." There went Halloween. "Or even a tooth fairy!"

"How'd you find out about the tooth fairy?" I asked, both amused and saddened by her sober little face.

"When I lost my last tooth, Mom forgot to put the money under my pillow and just handed it to me in the morning."

No easy transition from myth to reality here.

Giving her a hug, I said, "Never mind. I'm real, and you're real, and that's all that matters." Teasing, trying to make her smile.

A long silence. Then cautiously, "Grandma, is *Jesus* real?"

I tried to tuck my jaded old mind into her fresh, innocent one, to internalize her bewilderment as treasured childish fancies toppled about her. I felt angry at that moment with literature, the media, schools, parents—all who propagate the myths and then yank them away, creating the first questionings about adult integrity.

Most of all I resented the suspicions swirling about the only real superhero, Jesus Christ. If the rest all turned out to be fairy tales, why not the virgin birth, the miracles, the cross, and the Resurrection? Her simple question verified all my long-held objections to childhood's fantasy figures. If we are going to introduce them, let's at least label them with a clear line between myth and reality.

Long after she'd been assured by all of us that Jesus was indeed real, I still thought of her haunting little question. In spite of our quick response to the validity of Jesus, I wondered how real He was for us, the adults in the room.

Did we honestly believe that we must give an accounting to Him for all our thoughts and actions and that eternity depended upon that accounting?

Did we believe He would indeed return, splintering the firmament with a golden, glorious entry, replete with supernatural beings of a splendor beyond our earthbound imaginings?

Or have we watched the parade of pseudo outer space antics across our video screens so long that the King of the universe and all His holy angels simply join the procession?

Do our sophisticated voices form an echo to my granddaughter's candid question? Is Jesus real? Is Jesus real? Is Jesus . . .

"But what about you?" he asked. "Who do you say I am?" Simon Peter answered, "You are the Christ, the Son of the living God" (Matt. 16:15, 16).

A Gift for Lisa

It was a hectic summer. When I agreed to the deadline for the book upon which I was working, I had no idea how long it would take, or how many interruptions I would experience. I came to the place where I was working 12- to 14-hour days and going to bed with a headache every night.

The worst part is that friends and family simply do not understand. Even though you tell them, they think that writing is something that will somehow compress into whatever time you have, that you are making much ado over nothing.

Only my husband, who was feeding each day's output into the computer, knew the stress under which I was living. He did his best to help, protect, and encourage me.

At any rate, I was finding it extremely difficult to keep up with family activities. Our granddaughter Lisa's tenth birthday was coming up, and she had made a wish list from which I could do my shopping. Her aunt Amy and I had taken a Sunday afternoon to find the jean jacket that was top priority. We had also picked up a couple of small items, but I still wanted to get her one more thing and wasn't sure what it should be. Nothing on the list seemed quite right.

Another afternoon I raced into town to pick up an anniversary gift for friends, and as I drove away from the store I began to pray, "Lord, I keep having this feeling there's something else I need to buy for Lisa, but I just don't have time to search through all the stores. Please guide me quickly to something meaningful that she'll enjoy."

Even as I was praying, the clear direction came to my mind, "Turn here." As I was well into the intersection, I made a hasty scan of the surrounding traffic and whipped my car into a right turn, still wondering why. This street led directly away from the shopping center. But then I knew. It did lead to a small Christian bookstore on the edge of town.

OK. God wanted me to purchase something at the Christian bookstore. (This was beginning to be fun.) What? A tape, perhaps? She loves music.

I entered the tiny store and headed for the tapes, but the selection was extremely limited and I failed to see anything I thought she'd like or didn't already have.

Scanning each item, I moved slowly about the room. A picture for her bedroom? Nothing appropriate. A book? I'd already purchased a book.

Next a small display of Bibles. Suddenly I laughed to myself. How come I had been so dense? It should have been my very first thought for her birthday. Lisa's family does not attend church, but several months ago God spoke to Lisa's heart in a unique way, and she responded. Since then she has been attending church quite faithfully all by herself. I am so proud of her. With the greatest joy, I examined carefully all the children's Bibles and finally chose a pale-blue Precious Moments version of *The Living Bible*. It was easy reading and had interesting helps.

As I drove home, my heart was full of praise to God, who was willing to lead His thoughtless daughter to what should have been the obvious gift.

As Lisa sat beside me in church the next Sabbath, carefully looking up the pastor's texts, I was not only grateful that God stooped to hear my hurried prayer in the thick of traffic, but also so very thankful that His eye was upon this dark-haired child beside me. What were His dreams for her? Why had He spoken to her so clearly that she rose and dressed on Sabbath morning while the rest of her family slept or went about their secular activities?

I too must guard her carefully. I must be alert to all her spiritual needs. *Help me when I'm blind, Father. Give me spiritual eyesalve, as you did this week. Together we'll make Your dream come true.*

For the eyes of the Lord are on the righteous and his ears are attentive to their prayer (1 Peter 3:12).

Are You Listening, Lord?

Jean sat beside me in a painting class. We didn't know each other especially well but enough so that we shared paints and fretted together when we couldn't keep up with the instructor. It was hard to tell her age. In her soft pink angora sweater, she looked maybe 45.

She didn't look any different this particular afternoon from all the other days we'd painted together. But *she* was different. She was doing battle with slavery.

As the instructor announced, "That's it for today," my artist friend threw down her brush and began to scrabble about hastily among the items in her purse, searching for cigarettes. When she finally had one lit, I noticed her hands were shaking badly.

"I'm trying to quit," she said, inhaling deeply and laughing as she realized the incongruity of her explanation against its smoky backdrop. "If I hadn't gotten this thing into my mouth when I did, I think I'd have punched someone, or at least tipped the table over."

"Have you been a heavy smoker?" I asked.

"Three to five packs a day for 25 years," she replied. "A couple of years ago I quit for six months. They say if you can make it through three days, the worst is over, but after all those weeks if I saw other people lighting up in a car when I was driving, I'd find myself nearly crashing into them. My husband said I'd better go back to smoking before I had an accident. He didn't have to tell me twice."

"So what prompted you to try quitting again?"

"I've developed some health problems that my doctor refuses to treat unless I stop smoking, so I have no choice. This is my fourth cigarette today, and I'm just about crazy."

She was attending a class sponsored by the American Cancer Society and was hesitant to go that evening for fear she'd be the only one who'd failed.

"You certainly haven't failed," I encouraged. "To go from four packs to four cigarettes in one day is real progress. You just hang in there and back off to three tomorrow. Drink lots of fruit juice, and when you feel like smoking, get out and walk or ride your bike instead."

"I'm praying," she sighed. "Just praying I'll make it."

"I'll pray with you," I said softly, and we were faster friends than we had been before.

I can't get her out of my mind. I think about her slavery, for that's what bad habits are. I have some of my own, not as lethal as nicotine, but just as binding.

I spoke to the Great Emancipator in behalf of all of us slaves:
Oh, Lord, set us free.
We both love and loathe our vices.
Are You listening, Lord?
You've said, "Come boldly to the throne of grace."
You must not brush us aside.
You are our only hope.
We cannot be patient.
We are dying self-inflicted deaths over which we have no control.
Hear our cries.
You have promised that the truth shall make us free.
We must hold You to that vow.
We need the healing now. Amen.

Answer me speedily, O Lord; my spirit fails! (Ps. 143:7, NKJV).

Do We Hear His Voice?

A small group of us had gathered for prayer meeting. There's something precious about prayer meeting, because those who care enough to put aside their secular interests midway through the week and refresh their friendship with their Lord form a very special bond. Some had traveled a good distance, and we rejoiced to be together.

We sang a hymn and opened our Bibles to the sixth chapter of Romans. Our pastor said to a young man near the front, "Ray, would you start with verses 1 through 4? We like to hear your voice."

Now, our pastor is Indonesian, and sometimes he expresses himself in the English language (which he speaks fluently) a little differently than an American would. I suppose you or I would have said to Ray, who is not a church member and does not always attend prayer meeting, "Would you read the first four verses? We're so happy to have you here tonight." But Pastor Jim's "We like to hear your voice" was so much better.

It made me suddenly very conscious of voices. As various persons read Paul's rich oratory I thought how dear indeed were the individual voices and how I would have recognized each one anywhere on earth, though I were blindfolded.

I thought also of our six children, all now away from home. Some a continent away. Others only a few miles. But when the phone rings and each one says, "Hi, Mom," that child does not need to be identified further, for my ear recognizes instantly which one is calling.

I recalled how startled I had been years before when first listening to a tape of stories I had recorded for our children's entertainment. My own voice had been that of a stranger, though it did not seem so to the children.

Somehow our own speech does not register in our brain in the same way as it does to those listening. Thus a recording of our voice is unsettling, like catching a reflection of ourselves in a store window and for a second seeing just another stranger on the street. For some reason, we do not "know" our own voice in the same comforting, familiar way we recognize the voice of others.

Which brings me to a collection of Bible verses that are among my favorites. In the tenth chapter of John, Jesus talks to the Pharisees about His role as the good shepherd and His relationship with His sheep.

He says the sheep "hear his voice" and "he calleth his own sheep by name" (verse 3, KJV); and the sheep "follow him: for they know his voice" (verse 4, KJV).

For many years I've counted myself as one of the Lord's sheep, but I wonder whether His voice is as familiar and dear to me as the voice of my family and friends.

You say, Well, that's asking quite a bit. After all, God's hardly around the block from your house and mine.

True. But He said the sheep "know" His voice and "follow."

So I expect it's possible, in some mysterious spiritual way, to recognize His promptings clearly. There have been times when I've enjoyed that sweet experience. Usually when I've been living very close to Him over a long period. Then I do feel His presence as close as any friend's, and it brings me real pleasure to respond to His biddings.

But there are also periods when I feel nothing. I'm so frighteningly a part of this world, caught up in housecleaning and socializing and a lot of other things that seem essential. I don't hear His voice at all. Or maybe I do—faintly—through my busyness, but I brush it aside, not having time or even inclination to "follow."

How can that be? For His shepherding is everything. It neutralizes all the bleakness of this world. His voice is the one sane, loving, dependable factor on a planet gone mad. It's utter folly to tune it out. The silence is filled with danger.

But the Shepherd does not give up easily. He cherishes each sheep in a special way, just as my heart delights in each of my children. He continues to call and urge the stragglers back to the flock. Some will reject that tender voice until it no longer falls in familiar tones upon their ears. The patient concern will become offensive. But for those who respond there's a magnificent promise.

"My sheep hear my voice, and I know them, and they follow me: And I give unto them eternal life; and they shall never perish, neither shall any man pluck them out of my hand" (verses 27, 28, KJV).

O Lord, shepherd me most of all when I turn away. Pick me up and carry me in Your arms if need be, but never let me stray beyond the sound of Your voice. Amen.

Today, if you hear his voice, do not harden your hearts (Heb. 3:7, 8).

Words That Heal

The name of Hanan Mikhail-Ashrawi has come to my attention several times of late. She is probably the most prominent woman in the Arab world—an articulate voice among the new Palestinians. Raised in an upper-class Christian home, she is the youngest of five daughters. In 1967 Israel seized her hometown of Ramallah. Though safely ensconced at the American University of Beirut, she lived with concern for her family and their home, which she was not to see for seven years. In her grew a determination to bring such turmoil to an end. Today she has her admirers and her critics as she works for freedom and peace in the Palestinian cause. She's sometimes accused by her own people of courting the limelight, but the West finds her bright, educated, and honest.

For some reason this woman intrigues me. She is strong and determined, and if she enjoys power a bit too much, I can forgive that. I suppose the thing I admire most about her is her facile tongue.

Probably her greatest asset today lies in her language skills. Johanna McGeary, writing in the May 25, 1992, issue of *Time*, describes them thus:

"Words, and a dagger-sharp talent for choosing the right ones to turn tired propaganda into poignant exhortations or make diplomatic doublespeak sound incisive, are Hanan's stock in trade. Her colleagues at Bir Zeit University, where she taught English literature for 17 years, were always awed, and often overruled, by her command of the language. She could outtalk them as well in Arabic as in English. She has a good ear for saying the right thing the right way, says a member of the peace delegation—not talking, as Palestinians are wont to do, out of two sides of her mouth, but shaping a single message to penetrate the preconceptions of different listeners. She also has a talent, aggravating to her rivals, for expressing a position better than the person who created it. 'She knows,' says one of her critics, 'that language is a major ingredient in making a public figure today.' "

Words are important to me, too, not just because they are the tools of my trade, but because with them one is able to influence the thinking of others. The best authors understand that writing is more than stating facts. There must be a cadence to every line, and each word must fit into its slot as delicately as the last piece of a puzzle.

Probably the most critical words, however, are those that fall spontaneously from our lips. If the writer puts upon paper (or into a computer) harsh and hurting words, they can be erased, but those words that seem to leap from our mouths—almost of their own accord—cannot be eradicated.

James and Solomon both had some pretty sober comments about the tongue.

"If anyone considers himself religious and yet does not keep a tight rein on his tongue, he deceives himself and his religion is worthless" (James 1:26). "No man can tame the tongue. It is a restless evil, full of deadly poison" (James 3:8).

It's interesting that whereas James calls the tongue a "restless evil," Solomon says that "the tongue of the righteous is choice silver" (Prov. 10:20). He also says: "The lips of the righteous nourish many" (verse 21) and "The mouth of the righteous brings forth wisdom" (verse 31), and "The tongue of the wise brings healing" (Prov. 12:18).

So we must assume that James's gloomy prediction that no one can control the tongue is spoken in the context of our natural sinful state. But when we allow that hopeless condition to be invaded by the Holy Spirit, the tongue becomes an instrument of nurture and wisdom. Praise God for divine intervention! May our words today bring healing as did the words of Jesus. "No one ever spoke the way this man does" (John 7:46).

Reckless words pierce like a sword, but the tongue of the wise brings healing (Prov. 12:18).

How Much Is $50,000?

Hunched over the kitchen table in the dim light of a kerosene lamp, I perused the Sears catalog in search of a new dress. At 10 years of age, I had seldom experienced the pleasure of a ready-made dress.

My grandmother, with whom I lived, was offering counsel. More specifically, she was discouraging me from choosing an elaborate silk concoction for which I'd have little use in rural Vermont. She opted for a dark-green tailored dress with a white lace collar, too severe for a child. Neither of us was right, but would it be years before I understood that.

We debated a little testily over the decision until the third occupant of the room intervened. He was not a member of the family, but a guest. He was known in our neck of the woods as "the dynamiter." My grandfather, the town road commissioner, when building a new road occasionally employed the dynamiter to come with his equipment and remove some ledge of stubborn granite that was impeding progress. When this necessity arose, the demolition expert was a guest in our home for whatever length of time it took for the work to be completed. He was a man of few words, and I stood somewhat in awe of him.

This particular evening as my grandmother and I haggled over the catalog purchase, our guest listened and smoked his pipe. Finally he spoke decisively. "Young lady, if you are fortunate enough to purchase a new dress in these hard times [the country was just limping out of the Depression], you'd best listen to your grandma and order what she sees fit."

I was so aghast to be reprimanded by this stranger that I spoke no further word in my own defense, and the matronly green dress was promptly ordered. But the gentleman was not finished. "Two years ago I inherited $50,000 from a relative who died, but I have not gone on any spending sprees. It's in the bank for a rainy day, and I live as thriftily as possible. Be thankful for the necessities of life, child, and don't be worrying your folks with fancy ideas."

I was speechless with humiliation and wide-eyed with wonder. When he rose to go to his room a short time later, I barraged my grandmother with questions.

"How much is $50,000?"

"Is he rich?"

"How long will it take to spend it all?"

Gram smiled at my greedy curiosity. Yes, $50,000 was a great deal of money. Yes, he was rich (in those days he really was).

"Then why does he work?"

"Because he's a wise man and knows work has more benefits than just monetary rewards."

"Like what?" I turned the pages of the catalog slowly, savoring what I'd do with $50,000.

"Well, one is much healthier, both physically and mentally, when working. God gave work to men and women as a blessing and to keep them out of mischief."

"If I had $50,000, I'd certainly not work. And I'd buy something from every page of this catalog," I said.

My grandmother held her peace, but it was not the last she was to hear of the matter. Hardly a day passed in which I didn't muse, out loud, about our guest's great good fortune. It wasn't fair. How come he dressed like any ordinary man and did such dirty work? If I had just a tiny portion of his windfall, I could have a wardrobe that would be the envy of my friends for miles around.

Finally Gram wearied of my immature prattle and sat me down for a lecture on our long front porch. "Now, I want you to listen to me," she admonished, "and then let's hear no more about that $50,000. You *are* rich. Do you understand?"

I shook my head that I did not.

"You are a part of God's family, thanks to Jesus. *That* is wealth. You are dearly loved by your gramp and me. *That* is wealth. You have a searching, observant mind, and the ability to describe on paper all that you think and feel and see. *That* is a gift worth far more than $50,000. You take a special kind of joy in life because you experience more than most of us. You should not envy any other human being . . . ever!"

I hung my head and did not respond. For the first time I glimpsed my own good fortune and the high privilege of creativity. Everything was important. The good experiences and the bad. They were all part of my wealth. Maybe someday I'd even write about the ugly green dress.

I looked up to say thanks, but Gram had already melted back into the routine of her day, not daring to hope I'd accepted my legacy.

I have learned the secret of being content in any and every situation (Phil. 4:12).

How to Behave in a Riot

Thumbing through *Time*, I flipped past a colorful riot photo without interest, barely seeing. I was tired of riots. Of demonstrators. Of faces filled with rage. I realized, with wonder, that I was no longer stunned by streets littered with hats, shoes, clubs, and the dead and dying. It was a familiar sight offered up frequently by a sensation-glutted media. I did not understand people who went out into the street, hitting and yelling until blood flowed and life trickled away.

I forced myself to go back and really look at the photo. The riot happened to be in Manila. It could have been anywhere. Three dead men lay in the deserted street, one so close I could count the stripes on his blue sneakers. Facedown on the pavement, he sprawled awkwardly, like a rag doll tossed aside by a bored child.

Then I saw his hand, his left hand. Long-fingered, well-manicured, bearing a simple gold wedding band, it was the hand of a scholar, an artist. It didn't belong in the littered street. It should have sprung from a fine white shirt and expensive wool suit. It was the hand of a sensitive, intelligent man.

Suddenly the Philippine street took on reality. The three men were sons of God whose deaths represented a terrible waste, a pitiful misunderstanding of God's purposes for them. And now they had no remaining options. One would like to think that they set out upon their mission with only peaceful intentions, but the iron rods and clubs with nails protruding precluded such a conclusion. With violence, if necessary, they surged forth to make their point. And the young man with the beautiful hands paid a high price.

A long time ago another young Man opened His hands against the rough wood of a cross, submitting to the brutality of rioters screaming, "Crucify Him, crucify Him!" But what a difference in the deaths. Jesus of Nazareth volunteered to die so that the young Filipino, should he choose, might live—that every man might live—eternally. He faced the angry mob with calm submission because He valued life. Because every human was important to Him. Because He abhorred war and rioting.

He taught a quaint and gentle religion, startling, often disappointing to those of His day. He told His followers that when the Romans ordered them to carry their luggage one mile, they should carry it two. If one's coat was demanded, give one's shirt also. He made no attempt to right the evils of the world, but instead taught men and women to meet injustice with meekness and tender concern for their oppressors.

We may never be caught up in the mass hysteria of a riot—though Americans are certainly not immune to such madness—but the principle applies to a thousand less-colorful situations in the home, at the office, in the factory, on campus.

Our so-called rights are frequently threatened. We are misunderstood, blamed unjustly, maligned, taken advantage of. It's all part of the tangled network of sin in which we function, but *how* we react is an individual freedom. We can bludgeon with verbal clubs, or wield the "soft answer" that "turneth away wrath" (see Prov. 15:1, KJV). We can press for all that's due us, or ignore our "rights." Done out of fear and with resentment, this could be degrading, but done voluntarily, from a sanctified heart, the result is a splendid peace known only to the Master's own.

While the world riots and hate reigns, let those of us who serve Him demonstrate the awesome power of His love.

Your attitude should be the same as that of Christ Jesus: who, being in very nature God, did not consider equality with God something to

be grasped, but made himself nothing, taking the very nature of a servant, being made in human likeness. And being found in appearance as a man, he humbled himself and became obedient to death— even death on a cross! (Phil. 2:5-8).

Nothing but a Slang Word?

Amy and I sat at our dining room table as we stuffed manicotti for an evening of holiday entertaining. We were nearly at the end of our things-to-do list, so we chatted idly and watched the birds come and go at the feeder. Chickadees hopped cheerfully about, and cardinals were red as blood against new-fallen snow.

All at once, out of the corner of my eye, I saw a large bird drop out of the sky and settle with a peculiar fluttering motion onto the snow beneath the feeder. I had seen a host of birds throughout my country days—blue jays, nuthatches, thrashers, juncos, grosbeaks, assorted woodpeckers, indigo buntings, and many more. This was a hawk. Small, smooth, and gray, with a very prominently marked chest.

"I've never seen a hawk near the feeder," I exclaimed delightedly. "This hard winter must have driven it to desperation."

"Looks like a dove to me," Amy commented. Birds, a part of her world since childhood, interested her about as much as a snowdrift at the back door.

"That's it! That's exactly what he looks like. Must be a pigeon hawk. I've never seen one before." I grabbed the bird book from the window-sill and scrabbled through the index. There it was on the color plate. A pigeon hawk for sure, or in its more authentic old English, a merlin. Well, a high day indeed. It sat quite still upon the snow, as though patiently waiting for me to check each identifying feature. *There is something in the eye of a hawk*, I thought, *that repels despite my pleasure at adding a new bird to my list.*

Suddenly, with a thrust of power, the hawk lifted from the earth and soared off beyond the treetops into the clear blue winter sky. Amy and I gasped in unison and leaped toward the window, for from its claws hung—in all its bright, feathered beauty—a limp, red cardinal.

All the time that it had been sitting there so quietly, allowing me to admire its fine markings, it had been doing its deadly work beneath its outspread wings. I went from ecstacy to anger. The gentle, showy cardinals were my special joy. How could that little hawk, hardly bigger than its prey, have committed such an act of cruelty? It must have pounced upon the unsuspecting victim in that first moment when it was briefly below my line of vision.

All that evening when I ate and laughed and played games with guests, I could not shake the memory of bright-red feathers hanging from curved talons. I suppose the act was simply a natural part of the hawk's survival, but I hated it. I hated the ugliness of sin, all its pain and fear and bloodshed.

Later, in *People* magazine, I saw a survey that attempted to determine what acts today's citizens labeled sin, if any. A reader wrote: "I was astonished to see what is essentially an archaic religious concern (i.e., 'sin'), appropriate and consequential only to the Pilgrims or the Bible, on the pages of *People*. . . . To me the phrase, 'It's a sin' became strictly a slang expression years ago."

I thought of sin in the natural world, afflicting innocent creatures, and then of sin among humans, so prevalent that some no longer even acknowledge the term as valid. I thought of my own long personal struggle against it. I longed for that day when humans will no longer be polled for their definitions of sin and cardinals will no longer die.

Therefore, dear friends, . . . be on your guard so that you may not be carried away by the error of lawless men and fall from your secure position (2 Peter 3:17).

Peonies and Priorities

Before me sits a huge vase of peonies, and all the room is awaft with their fragrance. Eleven are deep rose in color, and two pure white. I was going to say they were exquisite, but exquisite is not the word for peonies. Peonies are big and showy and dramatic, and this collection, corralled in a clear Italian glass vase, is absolutely breathtaking. (While I am trying to write, my eyes keep creeping back toward them. It's a problem I have with beautiful things. Sometimes I have to retreat to a dim corner of my office where all I have to view is two dark-paneled walls. I think I could look at these peonies all day, marveling at their texture and hue as shifting light touches them at different angles.)

The peonies were a gift. A gift from a treasured friend, a sister in Christ. Outside of our brief weekly greeting in church, we do not see each other often. We are both busy women, busier than we should or would like to be. But once each summer she goes to her extensive peony collection, cuts an armful of choice blooms, and drives them to my house. Eloise is not a gardener. The peonies were already planted at her home when she and her husband purchased it many years ago, and such is the nature of these plants that they bloom prolifically still. But Eloise knows *my* passion for flowers, and so she sets aside a morning in which she brings her annual gift. We tour my gardens (even though she's not a gardener, her mother was, so she has an appreciation of flowers), and we chat. In the hour or two we spend together I realize all over again how much we have in common, how I enjoy her quick wit and soft-spoken manner. I am sadly aware of our loss in not spending more time together, in not sharing at deeper levels.

But we are foiled by busyness. She spoke today of the work factor in her life, of how work had consumed her since youth and of how she was scheming to slow down, all the time fearing it was impossible. Her years have been full and challenging. She and her husband ran a small airport until retirement. I'm always amazed that this petite, quiet woman is perfectly capable of getting into a plane and heading off into the blue.

Perhaps we enjoy each other because we're the kind of women who did the things we wanted to do instead of just dreaming about them. We've moved beyond our comfort zones and tried scary things. We've worked very hard and had fun. But now we are older, and it's becoming difficult to keep pushing the boundaries, yet people expect it of us, and we, quite unconsciously, keep expecting it of ourselves.

I think there is a good time ahead for us, however. I sensed this morning that Eloise was making some firm decisions about the future, and I have been doing the same. It is time to slow down and, instead of being apologetic about our more relaxed pace, to announce it and enjoy it. I am looking forward to putting boxes of snapshots into albums, spending time with my grandchildren, cooking more healthful meals, helping Don with the vegetable garden—all things my frantic schedule over the past 20 years has denied me.

Most of all I desire to nurture my already sweet relationship with Jesus. I want to know Him in every way humanity is allowed to know Him. I count *that* the last, most exciting project of my life. Eloise and I share that goal. The peonies will bloom each year with or without her help. That's how peonies are. I expect we'll find a lot of other things do fine without us, too. And she and I will explore and grow in new and quieter ways, preparing for the greatest adventure of all, meeting our Lord at His coming.

"Martha, Martha," the Lord answered, "you are worried and upset about many things, but only one thing is needed. Mary has chosen what is better" (Luke 10:41, 42).

Antidote

I don't mind gray days in November, but by April I'm geared for daffodils and sunlight. Thus one spring morning as I traveled in a downpour along Interstate 90 between Rochester and Syracuse, New York, my mood was as grim as the lowering skies. Tired and pressured from all sides, I resented the errand that drew me from home. Then I resented my resentment, because usually life, with all its complexities, still seems a gift of startling wonder. The Land of Grim, for me, was foreign territory and definitely no tourist spot.

The radio offered a strident rock and roll group, a local talk show host expounding 15 ways to disguise leftover Easter ham, and on FM some very nervous violins (perhaps on a better day I'd have labeled them lively). At any rate, I found nothing across the dial to lift my spirits.

And then, right in the middle of my pity party, I came to the white silo with the yellow smiley face. Sitting upon a rise above the highway, it was big and bright and just what a smiley face should be—cheerful!

I had to smile back. I never can drive by it without smiling. And the minute I smiled I felt better. That big, silly, beaming face set everything straight. The irksome rain became only spring showers for the greening of lawns and the nudging of dormant bulbs. My head began to buzz with gardening plans, and I thanked God for life and vitality, and yes, even the duties of the day.

As I passed the friendly silo on my return trip, an old quote by Julia Seton popped into my head: "We have no more right to put our discordant states of mind into the lives of those around us, and rob them of their sunshine and brightness, than we have to enter their houses and steal their silverware."

27

It occurred to me that if a cheery face painted on a silo could reverse my mood for the day, we humans probably do have the power to rob one another of peace of mind, or, in a more positive vein, to share the gift of a happy heart. I analyzed those with whom I rub shoulders—the family, the neighborhood, the church, and a wide circle of friends. Indeed, there are some whose negative tendencies sometimes erode my normal state of content. But there are also those who see good in everything, whose wit and laughter enrich my days.

For even the gloomiest individual there is an antidote, however. When Jesus Christ and His mission become real to us, it's almost impossible to stay discouraged for long. But we must internalize the wonder and the excitement of it, really get hold of it, if we are to be set free of despondency. It requires us to shift our concentration from this world to a spiritual realm. To those of practical bent this may sound a bit too wispy for their taste, but there's nothing ethereal about it. Jesus is real, hands-on real. What He offers is real. A new life so that we can respect ourselves at last and best of all a new friendship with Him after all the years of separation. Now, that's enough to put a smile on every face, isn't it?

A gentle lady long ago wrote: "Every soul is surrounded by an atmosphere of its own—an atmosphere, [that] may be charged with the life-giving power of faith, courage, and hope, and sweet with the fragrance of love. Or it may be heavy and chill with the gloom of discontent and selfishness, or poisonous with the deadly taint of cherished sin. By the atmosphere surrounding us, every person with whom we come in contact is consciously or unconsciously affected" (*Christ's Object Lessons*, p. 339).

So let your joy in Jesus shine into the dark and discouraged lives about you, for, you see, even the smiley-face upon the barn reached farther than the farmer who painted it ever dreamed.

I will turn their mourning into gladness; I will give them comfort and joy instead of sorrow (Jer. 31:13).

The Dog That Went to K-Mart

It so happened that I sat one day, for about 20 minutes, in the entrance to our local K-Mart, waiting for a friend. When I arrived I noticed a medium-sized, nondescript dog pacing uneasily back and forth outside the glass door. I watched him, idly at first, then with genuine interest.

He was worried. It was evident in his stance and in his eyes. Especially in his eyes. Large, expressive, and intelligent, they registered his concern as truly as any human eyes could have done. Between pacings he stopped to view the shoppers inside, searching intently for that familiar figure beyond the walls of glass. (I thought of a time I'd waited for a daughter at a prearranged point in a strange city, fearing we'd had a communications breakdown. I could identify with Fido.)

Each time someone entered, the little dog attempted to squeeze through the open door, only to find a knee fending him off. I observed the human reactions to this persistent canine with growing interest. Some took the time to look into his sad eyes and offer a word of comfort. Others spoke irritably, giving him a firm shove. One teenage girl squatted beside him, took his face in her hands, and said, "Do you really want to go shopping at K-Mart so badly?"

Kindness did not comfort this dog, however; nor did impatience distract him. In fact, he hardly noticed the array of humanity coming and going about him. He obviously didn't have the temperament for waiting stoically as some dogs do. He hated every moment away from the one he loved, and made no attempt to hide it.

I began to be curious about the owner. A plump dowager who attended his every need and daily brushed his rough coat? A rascal of a boy with whom he'd grown up and with whom he was inseparable?

Eventually I grew weary of watching him and turned my attention elsewhere. Then suddenly I heard a sharp, joyous bark. Turning, I saw a total metamorphosis. Every muscle in the dog's body stretched taut and expectant. His eyes glittered with anticipation, and the ecstatic barks increased in volume.

Now I could see the object of all this affection. A tall man, probably in his late 30s, straight as an arrow, strode through the inner door and then the outer one. He spoke not a word to the dog, nor so much as glanced in his direction. I thought for a moment there must be someone yet to come, but the dog danced about the tall man in such a frenzy of delight that there could be no question. They moved toward a waiting pickup truck, the dog prancing proudly at his owner's side. When the man opened the truck door, the dog leaped in and sat tall and very much at home in the passenger's seat.

Though I had seen no display of affection on the owner's part, there was obviously a rare relationship between the two, one so sure and settled that it was not threatened by the owner's present lack of attention. Somewhere, at some point, they had developed an understanding that required no theatrics on the master's part. He was simply *there*—reliable, trusted, and worthy of adoration.

I thought about my long relationship with Jesus—how over the years I've come to know Him.

At times He seems to be far away, and I'm like the dog at the door, lonely and uneasy. Other times I sense His presence even though He doesn't really seem to be looking my way. Then I'm just happy to know He's around, and I simply rest upon experiences we've shared in the past and the beautiful promises of Scripture.

There are rare, beautiful moments when He's not only present but I know He's smiling right at me, aware of me, loving me. And those moments keep me waiting at the door. Someday I shall see the actual form, the dear face. And if He doesn't speak at once it's OK, for our friendship is old and true.

Unlike the dog, I shall not leap in ecstasy about Him, but rather fall in gratitude at His feet. My heart, however, will dance, for in His presence there is fullness of joy.

Though you have not seen him, you love him; and even though you do not see him now, you believe in him and are filled with an inexpressible and glorious joy (1 Peter 1:8).

Transformation

Arriving home from town with a carful of groceries and my mind on lunch preparations, I turned off the four-lane highway onto our country road. The day was February gray, with a great angry bank of cobalt snow clouds rolling in from the northwest.

I was glad my errands were completed and there would be no reason for me to leave the safe, warm confines of home for the remainder of the day. Suddenly the sun, as though escaping momentarily from captivity, broke through the gloom, gilding the earth. Stubbled cornfields turned to gold, and each bare tree stretched silver limbs against the dark winter sky. I gasped at what God had done with a few muted colors and a wandering sunbeam.

And He wasn't finished yet, for out of the stubble rose a flock of gulls, their bellies gleaming in the sunlight, fragments of silver fluttering against the blackness of storm. Before I could catch my breath, the truant sunbeam was captured and the moment gone. Back to reality. Back to boots and chapped hands; cold, sluggish cars; and dingy, depressing days. But I had seen this world transformed, if only for an instant.

The experience triggered two areas of thought that entertained me throughout the snowy afternoon. That fleeting moment of splendor lighting this old familiar habitat of mine was a thrilling reminder that you and I have the opportunity to explore someday the far reaches of heaven and on and on into a universe of beauty and mystery beyond our wildest imaginings.

The wonders there will surely eclipse my silver birds and golden fields. And the One who created the beauty here, marred and battered with sin as it now is, will be our tour guide. Just the thought of being near enough to touch Him, to hear His voice, to see His smile is a wonder beyond my human comprehension.

It is a joy so long delayed that it has become dreamlike in quality, not relinquished—oh, no—but elusive and fragile. When it becomes reality, when we're blinded with the glory of other creations, I'll take time to thank Him for silver birds in an earthbound past.

Then my thoughts took a more practical turn. I thought of people I had known, ordinary gray people who met Christ and blazed into glowing, creative, loving individuals, hardly recognizable as their former selves.

I guess the truth is we're *all* ordinary gray people until He touches us. His transformations in human lives are even more astonishing than in the natural world. I have watched the haughty become meek, heard the profane speak His name with tender awe, and seen the rough gentled by His love.

I've felt His hand on *me*, chiding, encouraging, comforting, leading me home. He is the sunlight who transforms us all, if we will allow Him, into the very best that we can be—into silver birds rising against the storm of sin. I praise Him for that here and now, with assurance that I shall praise Him face-to-face on a day of His choosing in a universe of His making. Will you join me?

No eye has seen, no ear has heard, no mind has conceived what God has prepared for those who love him (1 Cor. 2:9).

When the Night Grows Dark

This is the great fear of the Christian, to live on this planet without God. As I travel about our country, I meet many individuals who are bowed beneath just such anxiety. They are sure they have sinned beyond God's mercy. This burden has haunted their nights and drained the joy from their days.

A Christian lady once told me God had revealed to her that I was being used of Him, but that I was not one of His. She listed actual names of individuals who no longer walked with God, in fact had become His enemies, and said that I was among them.

I drove home from that encounter stunned, and blinded with tears. I poured out my pain into my husband's compassionate ear and tried to believe his comforting words. I had never felt anything but loyalty and love for the God I served. I had failed Him many times, but found hope in the cross and all that it represented.

How could I be an enemy of God and not even know it? I fell to my knees and poured out David's prayer from an agony I'd never known existed. "Cast me not away from thy presence; and take not thy holy spirit from me."

I faced the sunlit mornings haunted with the terrible words. For years I woke in the night with the pronouncement settling upon me like doom.

In time I slowly came to realize that though I was a sinner, I had never turned away from God, not even in my rowdy, careless teenage years. Upon my knees, I had one last, long talk with Him about it and laid it to rest—almost. Once in a while it still comes to terrify me in the long watches of the night, but then I place it all over again in God's hands.

What I have expressed here in a few paragraphs was one of the most painful experiences of my life, and it went on during a period of years. To wonder, month after month, if one has somehow wandered from God's presence is a fearful thing. Never did I understand David's cry so well.

And thus, when individuals come to me in that distressed state, I surely can identify with them. It is my great joy to tell them that God's mercy is wide and tender. Though they may have sinned outrageously, their very concern is evidence that His love still pursues them. Down upon our knees we wrestle the thing out—often shed tears—and then lay the matter to rest. If there are situations that must be made right, we pray for courage to take the necessary steps. And as we part, I remind them again that it's very hard to escape the presence of God, for He values each one of us as a treasured only-child, following patiently behind us, armed with every resource of heaven, ready to open His arms in forgiveness at the slightest sign of repentance.

So today, if a great gloom settled upon you as you awakened; if, like David, you felt abandoned by the One you once loved and served, open your Bible and read Lamentations 3:22, 23; Isaiah 41:10; 50:10; John 8:1-11; Psalm 51:1-12; Luke 19:1-9; and Psalm 86:1-7.

When it is very dark, one must go forward, with only the flickering candle of faith.

Cast me not away from thy presence; and take not thy holy spirit from me (Ps. 51:11, KJV).

Two Kids and a Canyon

I was inching along the Capilano suspension bridge in North Vancouver, British Columbia, as best I could, while the whole fragile structure was swaying from side to side. Two hundred thirty feet below, the Capilano River splashed over rocks and offered occasional glimpses of salmon struggling upstream, but who could look? Keeping my footing seemed top priority.

Suddenly the whole chain of stumbling tourists came to a halt as a tiny Asian girl halfway across the narrow span planted her feet stubbornly and looked up at her dad. "I'm not taking another step," she said firmly. "I'm tired of all this walking and falling."

I laughed right out loud. She'd expressed my sentiments exactly. Patiently her father half-dragged, half-carried her to the other end of the bridge.

One way or another, I made it too and sat down on the observation deck to watch the reactions of those who followed, while my husband did some exploring on nearby trails. It was then I spotted the second diminutive Asian lass. (Vancouver is rampant with these little dolls.) Probably no more than 3 years old, she was impatient to make the return trip across the canyon, whereas her parents wished to relax and look about a bit. Finally, wearying of her teasing, her dad said, smiling,

"Go ahead. Wait for us on the other side."

I looked at the man in astonishment. Could he possibly be serious? Did he really mean for this wee creature to cross those 450 feet of uneasy walkway alone?

Looking at it objectively, I realized nothing could really happen to her. The wire rope sides were higher than her head. But remembering the other tot's fears, I couldn't believe any child would consider a lone crossing, much less be allowed one. But she set out. Not fearfully. Matter-of-factly. When the bridge flew into one of its spasms, she simply clung to the side until it calmed. At the midpoint, she turned, scanned the crowd at our end for her parents, blew them a kiss, and trudged once more toward her destination.

Later, when Don and I had staggered back across, we saw her sitting on a log, placidly sucking her thumb as she awaited her parents' arrival.

I thought a lot about those two little ones and their approach to life. I admitted, reluctantly, that I had a lot more in common with the first child. I am apprehensive of nerve-jarring experiences, and have often wished during a rough air flight that I could just get off. Sometimes, also, on my spiritual journeying, I've been tired of all the walking and falling. I too have wished to go not one step farther. I'm not a hardy adventurer on either literal or spiritual wanderings. Thus something in the second girl's staunch attitude both rebuked and challenged me. I envied her pluck.

Then I thought about the fathers and their relationships with their daughters. Both girls had trusted their dads completely. One enough to express her fears and unhappiness, the other enough to set out alone, with paternal blessing, on a rather hair-raising experience. Each father had dealt with his daughter's request in loving recognition of her unique personality and needs. When one child proved apprehensive, even rebellious, that father provided firm, loving support. When the other grew fretful and impatient to be off, her dad gave her the freedom to go and grow. Both actions took place in an atmosphere of love and trust.

I would have preferred to identify with the hardy little explorer, but my Father knows His fearful daughter well, and leads me, with more patience than I merit, through the scary places.

Thank You, Lord, for loving each of us just the way we are.

I guide you in the way of wisdom and lead you along straight paths. When you walk, your steps will not be hampered; when you run, you will not stumble (Prov. 4:11, 12).

Beyond the Stained-Glass Windows

A minor emergency sent me to a strange service station in a small town. As I awaited repairs, my eyes leisurely scanned the tiny front office. I don't mind waiting. I enjoy scrutinizing every detail of unfamiliar surroundings. Better yet if there are people involved. And that morning there were a few—a little handful of middle-aged and elderly men whom I suspect congregated there daily to review politics, the weather, and the local gossip.

I had known such gatherings around potbellied stoves in the general stores of my mountain-country childhood. I understood their wry pronouncements interspersed with long silences and grunts. They did not seem to be inhibited by my presence. In fact, they ignored my female-stranger intrusion as readily as if I'd been a fly upon the wall. That was OK with me. All the better for observing.

The room contained the usual cigarette machine and pop dispenser. The men uttered an occasional oath. It was drab, dreary, and greasy, as service stations tend to be. Yet three things caught my attention. First, the small tank of goldfish, with water as clear as a mountain stream. Even the glass and chrome on the tank gleamed. Not far away a saucy red geranium stood in the window nodding to passersby. And on the wall behind the pop machine hung a picture of Christ praying in the Garden of Gethsemane.

I'm not sure why the picture so startled me, or how I knew instinctively that the person who had hung it was the same one who tended the fish and the plant.

As a teenage boarding-school student I'd felt the impact of that particular painting. It hung in the front of the school chapel, and during Friday evening vespers it was always spotlighted in the darkened room, while somewhere in the wings young voices sang, " 'Day is dying in the west; Heaven is touching earth with rest.' " Though giddy with youth, for those hushed moments I'd felt very close to that solitary figure among the olive trees. I sensed something had happened there far beyond my immature comprehension. I tried to believe it reached down the ages to a teenage girl who'd not yet found her footing. And I always fought back unexplainable tears.

And here I was in the dirty service station 35 years later, confronted once more with the Christ of the garden. I no longer had trouble believing His struggle there related to the salvation of June Strong. In fact, my every hope centered on that assurance. But this incongruous confrontation with the painting compelled me to consider another aspect of His many-faceted character.

As He hung above the profane men with their cans of Coke I was made aware that He truly had come for *everyone*. That however hard we might try to keep Him behind the stained-glass windows, He would escape us. He would be out there searching in the streets where men and women work and play with little thought of Him. He would sit beside them in the most unlikely places, waiting for that moment when in pain or loneliness they might turn to Him.

Take me, Lord, out beyond the stained-glass windows to where the war is being fought. Let me meet people where they are, that my Friend may heal their wounds. Let me not rest until there is blood upon my hands and dirt upon my clothing. Take me out of the chapel and into streets, lest I find in the end I never knew the Christ of the garden after all.

There will be more rejoicing in heaven over one sinner who repents than over ninety-nine righteous persons who do not need to repent (Luke 15:7).

We Can Wait

The preacher said all the right things. He told of all her goodness, her courage, her humor, her toughness, her gentleness. He read appropriate scriptures. She would have liked the dignity and simplicity of this memorial service, my friend Eunie, could she have heard it.

The church—her church—was packed. Of course. She had a rare talent for making you feel you were special. Not just special in general, but special to her. So all the people she had nurtured and loved and delighted were there, each mourning his or her loss in a different way, all sure they had shared a little bit of her unknown to the others. And perhaps they had, for she was many-faceted. She knew what we liked, how we lived, what we thought, each one of us. And she focused upon our uniqueness as though there were no other.

I remember her in so many ways. Reading her poetry, her fine, tight verse with a hint of mischief, because it was often sedately hilarious, though she was capable of pathos. I often found her painting, her watercolors capturing sunlight filtered through the rainbow hues of her glassware collection.

She had a fistful of ribbons won at art exhibits, but it wasn't the ribbons she cherished. It was beauty. And God let her play with beauty—words, watercolors, flowers. How she reveled in them all! But it was *people* she loved best, and she invested her time, her talents, and her energies in all of us. A note, a card, a phone call, a gift. An afternoon of labor for an ill friend. Once she brought primroses and planted them in my prayer garden while I was away, chuckling at the little mystery that would greet me when I returned. That's how she was.

Then, in the midst of her living and loving and giving, life began to cuff her around willy-nilly. Cancer dropped its dark shadow over her. She faltered momentarily, stunned and fearful, but came back fighting, refusing to bow to the aggressor. She laughed once more, putting darkness behind her, making light of chemotherapy and its attendant trials. There was a time of sunlight and hope.

But eventually the enemy struck again, ruthlessly, cruelly, unexpectedly. While she struggled against this new onslaught, she was hit by a car rounding a corner in the dusk, leaving her already frail body battered and broken. Most of us would have died in those terrible first weeks. But not Eunie.

With a triumphant tenacity she lived and fought her way back month by agonizing month, until at last she could take a few shuffling steps without her canes. A victorious moment. She crowed gleefully and expected us to cheer. And we did. Oh, we did. In this magnificent woman we saw humanity at its best. There was no giving up or giving in. Only a gratefulness for each new day and a splendid courage with which to meet it.

Chemotherapy again. Progress. Hope. We wanted her to be all right. She pretended, and we believed because we wanted it so much. So when she died, we were startled. Death had won after all, in spite of her courage, her trust, her tenacity. We could hardly grasp it.

For me her memorial service, however sensitively done, could be only a mockery. There was no balm for her loss, no eloquence to capture her essence.

In the pew in front of me a little girl wept quietly into her mother's coat sleeve throughout the service. I needed a coat sleeve too. And someone older and wiser inside it to tell me why. I wept inwardly for the things I'd never said to her and for her magic, which would never come again.

At the end, a bell, far off, tolled solemnly while we all sat in stillness. The sound was lonely and majestic and haunting, and all the tragedy of this planet's 6,000-year history passed before me as I listened. So many deaths, so many tears. A rolling mass of pain, snowballing down the centuries, with only a frail cross to stay its power. But in that cross I put my trust.

She'll rise again, and all that was Eunie will gladden not only the hearts of those who loved her, but also the heart of Him who knew the cross and absorbed its pain. He's not a spectator God, but a participant. Let the bell toll. Dry your tears, little girl. It's just a matter of time, and we can wait, you and I.

Let us hold unswervingly to the hope we profess, for he who promised is faithful (Heb. 10:23).

Without Words

In his book *Liberating Faith* Geoffrey Kelly talks about the discipline of the secret in the early apostolic church. According to Kelly, the ancient church avoided mention of baptism, Communion (or the Eucharist, as he called it), and the death and resurrection of Christ in the presence of unbelievers. The reason for this was twofold. First, it was to protect the name of Jesus and the symbols of the Christian church from mockery, but the second and more significant reason sprang from their belief that the Christian lifestyle should be the witness, rather than the words.

Somehow I couldn't let go of that concept. Suppose I could never speak of Christ or of what He had done for me. Nor of the doctrines of the church. Nor share a verse of Scripture that opened with new meaning like a Fourth of July sparkler. What if my only means of witness was my daily, very ordinary life?

It was a revelation to realize that probably I would be kinder, more quick to meet needs, more generous with my time. I would seek ways to show Christ, in all His beautiful unselfishness, to others. Maybe this discipline of the secret wasn't such a bad idea.

Not long ago in a large city to which I traveled to fill a speaking engagement, I met a young woman whom I shall not soon forget. Because of certain conditions in her childhood she did not learn to read and write as well as she would have liked. This handicap hindered her from gaining an education. She told me all this cheerfully, and then about her job, which, though menial, supported her.

We prayed together, and somehow she made me feel very loved. I was supposed to be the counselor, but this young woman did not need counseling. She was steady in the Lord and radiated a kind of innocent happiness that made me feel old and cynical.

When she rose to leave, she pressed a $10 bill into my hand. "I want you to buy something for your garden," she said. "Some lovely flower—red. I love red."

"I can't take this," I replied, thinking of her hard work and simple lifestyle. "You are so thoughtful, but I just can't take it."

I saw the hurt in her eyes. The bright face clouded. "It makes me so happy to think you will have a flower in your garden that will always remind you of my love. Please don't deny me that happiness."

I understood this was not a time to be noble. "Thank you, Sonia," I said. "I will look for the most beautiful flower I can find, to remind me of a beautiful lady."

This fall I ordered a deep-red lily called "Raspberry Fizz" (three of them to be exact), and when they bloom next summer I will remember a young woman who showed me a bit of Christ's love . . . simple, giving, uncomplicated. Sonia knows about the discipline of the secret.

Ellen White knew about it, too, though I doubt either she or Sonia ever heard the term. Years ago she wrote: "The unstudied, unconscious influence of a holy life is the most convincing sermon that can be given in favor of Christianity. Argument, even when unanswerable, may provoke only opposition; but a godly example has a power that it is impossible wholly to resist" (*The Acts of the Apostles*, p. 511).

I'm very thankful I'm free to speak of Christ to unbelievers, but I have a new vision of what it would mean to be mute for Him. Simply to love so intensely that hearts are melted and homesick for heaven. Maybe you and I should experiment with that ancient concept.

Let your light shine before men, that they may see your good deeds and praise your Father in heaven (Matt. 5:16).

It's OK to Be Scared Sometimes

I hadn't expected much of the recital—just the usual renditions of Bach and Beethoven, plus the ridiculous pleasure of hearing one's own perform with almost flawless precision. (Never mind that the practice sessions at home had nearly driven her siblings to mutiny!)

But as it turned out, sandwiched somewhere between the "Here-we-go, up-a-row" kids and the surprisingly competent teenagers, two adults—both of whom added something quite special to that otherwise ordinary afternoon—joined the roster of performers.

The small girl who struggled through "The Spinning Song" was followed by a gentleman of the same last name, obviously her father. We awaited eagerly the more professional piece he would surely render.

But folding his long legs awkwardly under the piano bench, he proceeded to play, rather nervously, a very simple piece from the beginner's book. The audience was amused but paid him the courtesy of straight faces. He walked gratefully back to his seat, grinned at his small daughter, and let out a great, audible sigh of relief. In that small act he freed us to chuckle—and chuckle we did.

He could laugh at himself. He was not so impressed with his adulthood that he could not become a beginner once more. Perhaps the simple tunes his daughter played had made his fingers itch to share her knowledge. He didn't just say, "Sure wish I'd had a chance to take lessons when I was a kid," but lifted the phone to add a new experience to his life. Neither did he duck the recital, but shared the apprehension and the excitement with that little one who'd probably begged, "Please, Daddy, you be in it too." He spoke to all of us of opportunities lost because of lethargy or foolish pride.

Later on, among the more advanced students, teenagers all, a lady arose (Mrs. Atwood, the program said) in a long white gown. The flowers in her hair highlighted her attractive face and trim figure. Again we were filled with anticipation. No beginner this one.

She played the first few measures of a lovely and spirited song—then appeared to repeat them. She stopped, sat quietly, then began to play something quite different, obviously from another movement of the piece. Well, some contemporary composers create very strange blends these days. Perhaps she was on course after all.

Then we noted the teacher hurrying down the aisle with her music. So she was in trouble. We were relieved when the familiar notes were placed before her. Now all would be well.

But all was not well. Once again the delightful opening enchanted us, but the music faltered and died away. She sat a moment, her hands resting on the keys, then turned on the bench to face us. (No running back to her seat in tearful confusion.) "I am too nervous to play for you," she said in a very winning, unself-conscious way. "I hope you will forgive me."

She was as relaxed as if we were family and the auditorium her living room. A wave of gentle laughter rippled over the audience, encompassing her in our compassion. Of course we forgave her. More than that, we loved her for trusting us to understand. She had saved us embarrassment by her lack of it. She had touched the vulnerability of each of us by saying it's OK to be scared sometimes. Fellow humans can accept our failures as well as our successes. We are siblings in our humanity.

The kids were good that day, but those two pioneering adults literally stole the show.

Let's trust and encourage each other. In so doing, we'll extend the loving acceptance of Jesus throughout our sometimes scary world.

Let the beloved of the Lord rest secure in him (Deut. 33:12).

Grounded!

Our family room overlooks a scene so tranquil it's easy for us to forget the hurly-burly of twentieth-century living. The lawn behind the house slopes, green and rolling, down to the pond and surrounding meadow.

One foggy October dawn, as the mists slowly lifted, I saw what looked like a Canada goose on the shore. But it couldn't be. Geese fly over our farm in thin, high, wavering wedges, but they never, absolutely never, land on our water. Too deep, we've been told. Waterfowl prefer shallow ponds for feeding.

A look through binoculars, however, confirmed my initial conclusion. It was a Canada goose—all by itself on the bank of our miniature lake.

Closer observation convinced us it had been nicked by a hunter but that only the second joint in one wing was broken. It could lift its great wings and flex them grandly, but the left one drooped a little toward the tip.

I couldn't bear the thought that the goose would never fly again. Perhaps it was only a wound that would heal, and it would join its kin in warmer climes before snow hurled itself across our blizzard-prone corner of the earth. But the days turned into weeks, and the left wing remained slightly out of kilter. The goose made no attempt to fly.

I realized this magnificent creature of the skies was now confined to earth, nothing more than a common barnyard fowl and undoubtedly doomed to death from starvation or exposure. Unless we stepped in to help.

I began to make phone calls. First to the veterinarians, who said wildlife was not their business. Then to conservationists, who sent me to the wildlife refuge, where the personnel hedged and squirmed. That Canada goose just didn't seem to be anyone's responsibility, but day by day it was becoming mine.

We carried dried corn from our garden to Charlie (the name we decided on), while I continued to harass everyone in the county who was supposed to be dedicated to the preservation of wildlife. Mostly they told me I could not fence or shelter the goose because it was against the law. But it wasn't against the law for a hunter to ground Charlie forever or for him to starve or freeze.

Finally a biologist with a heart, and a thick German accent, advised me to feed him, enjoy him, and with a little luck domesticate him. Domesticate! . . . What a sad ending for a creature who had traversed the skies, viewing with regal detachment the squares of green and brown below.

When I took Charlie corn I talked to him, but he always eased into the water, honking uneasily. On occasion our dog, who never did quite understand what the goose was doing there, chased him, sending him into an absolute panic. So mostly we kept our distance, but I was aware of him all day long.

He was not going to suffer. That much I had determined. We made plans for a shelter and an automatic feeder for the winter months. I wished he could know he was not alone with his problems.

One morning when sunlight was just creeping over the corn patch on the hillside beyond the pond, I noted that Charlie was not huddled down in the long grass under the dock, and neither was he alone. There were eight or 10 geese grazing about him, as content as if they had arrived for the winter. Why had they come? To lend aid to a fallen brother? Out of curiosity? Enticed by Charlie's corn? Would they stay? The answer to that one was no, for by full daylight they had lifted, wheeled in a graceful arc over the pond, and become only specks of black against the pinkness of sunrise. Charlie lifted his head as they rose, and he watched them circle above him, watched until there was nothing more to see. I watched with him, a lump in my throat as big as a walnut. I felt every ounce of his hurt.

But he had *me*. He wouldn't go hungry or cold, and even my friendship was available to him. He might like it better than goose friendship if he'd give it a fair try. He simply had to learn to trust me.

Occasionally I find myself grounded, for one reason or another. Grounded spiritually or emotionally, that is. Like Charlie's, my problem seems overwhelming and hopeless. I get totally zeroed in on it. The fact that God is providing for me abundantly and trying, in every way, to get my attention doesn't register because of my inward focus.

I learned something from Charlie that day. I learned that while I'm nursing my despair, on the shore there's Someone wonderful holding out the bread of life. Why is it so hard to remember that?

Why are you downcast, O my soul? Why so disturbed within me? Put your hope in God (Ps. 42:5, 6).

Turning Points

I held the letter in my hand and smiled through my tears. She had written, our 18-year-old daughter. "Graduation is two weeks away, and it seems everything I do has a certain 'last time' quality about it. My heart is heavy, and it's an awful feeling. I don't know what's the matter with me."

She attended a Christian boarding school some distance from home, and the friends she had made there had become almost family. She faced one of life's turning points, but knowing her, I felt sure she would deal with it despite the pain.

Truth was, I was struggling with a turning point of my own, and the tears I'd shed were as much for myself as for her. I'd heard all about the empty-nest syndrome, but as far as I was concerned, it was only a silly term for a silly situation experienced by women who had concentrated all their time and talents on child-rearing instead of keeping their lives balanced with a wide variety of interests.

Anyhow, by the time the youngest of our six went away to boarding school, the older ones were finished and back home living and working, so I didn't see much sign of an empty nest in my immediate future.

Meanwhile I was scribbling away furiously, trying to make up for lost time in a long-delayed writing career. At times I longed for less bedlam and more solitude. When the first ones left I hardly noticed, so busily was I juggling the duties of my hectic days. Besides, most of them didn't go far and were still often in and out of the home. We gathered for birthdays and holidays, and my writing career flourished like a radish in May.

But there came a September when the house fell silent. They were all gone. Three of them on the West Coast, thousands of miles from the old white farmhouse that had sheltered so many so long. Even the ones close by had become more and more involved in their own lives, less in need of home ties.

Ducks still sailed serenely around on the pond in the fall sunlight, colorful birds flashed in and out of the feeder, and the red leaves of autumn fell lazily onto manicured lawns. Our parakeet jabbered his nonsense during all my kitchen activities, and I found plenty of time to write. Perfect setting for the final third of my life! Except that my daughter's description of her own turbulent emotions could have described mine just as well. I too felt awful and didn't know what was the matter with me.

It took a young friend to diagnose my affliction. She labeled it "empty-nest syndrome." It could not be! Surely she was wrong. But every now and then I did find myself just walking around the house, crying for no reason whatsoever except that the world in which I lived was a great green lovely park where no children ever came to play. I'd see them coming up the hillside with bowls of wild raspberries picked along a hedgerow, or they would be racing down the driveway with a collie nipping playfully behind. But they were just mirages. It was over and done, and I must deal somehow with the remainder of my life and these unexplainable episodes of tears.

So because I like rules, I created some pertaining to this strange situation in which I found myself.

1. I would not dwell upon the past, calling to mind the happy events of yore. I would accept the fact that the mothering phase of my life was at an end. As evidence of my resolve I would redecorate the children's rooms (all of which were the worse for wear) and turn them into guest rooms. If the tears came, I would not deny them. They were legitimate grief for the loss of a great happiness and would abate in time.

2. I would concentrate on the advantages of this new phase of my life, getting outside more, spending more time with my husband, and being grateful I didn't have four or five lunches to pack daily.

3. I'd concentrate on enjoying my children as adults, instead of mourning the loss of their younger days. God willing, I'd keep my mind alert through study, work, and a growing friendship with God, so that they would look forward to my visits instead of relegating me to the nostalgic corners of their lives.

While our daughter faces an early turning point in her long journey, I struggle with one of the last in mine. May neither of us mourn the past overmuch, lest we miss the challenges and joys of the unfolding future.

There is a time for everything, and a season for every activity under heaven (Eccl. 3:1).

With God in the Garden

There's something about summer evenings. I hurry through the supper dishes to go outside to get a little work in before dark. I water a few newly planted Japanese irises, trim a rowdy rosebush, prune a small evergreen. Easy, end-of-the-day jobs.

Then, enjoying the variety of leaf and flower, I stroll through the gardens. A Pristine rose, so perfect in its unfurling that it takes my breath away. It's rare to find a rose these days that has not been marred, at least faintly, by one insect or another. But this one has achieved perfection. Its soft pearly pink will fade, in a few hours of strong sunlight, to nearly white, but here tonight in the dusk it's an indescribable hue. My hand moves toward it, touching Eden. Eve-like, I say to God, "This is it, the most beautiful bloom I have ever seen. You have outdone Yourself!"

And God smiles, because even God likes appreciation. My delight is His joy. For a moment, maybe it's Eden for Him, too.

I sit down on a bench in our new shade garden, where a blue delphinium towers higher than my head. The two benches, which Don and I gave each other for our forty-fourth wedding anniversary, are sheltered from view by a tall blue spruce and a huge boulder. Every time I look at the rock I think about it being underground for hundreds, perhaps thousands of years. It was dug from a farmer's field across the way. We hired a front-end loader and operator to bring it across the road and place it just where we wanted it. I think about the Indian feet that passed over it, the pioneer feet and the early settlers' plows whose blades dulled against its immovable spine. But now the rains have washed it clean. It sits beneath the clear blue sky and grows warm with the heat of the sun. It is a strong fortress in the tiny corner where on summer evenings I sit. Somehow it seems as precious as the rose.

This morning a tiger swallowtail butterfly came to a stand of jasione as I was working nearby. It was fairly drunk with ecstasy over the find. Jasione is not my favorite flower, but it was certainly that butterfly's. So greedily was it dining that it had no sense of my presence, and not only could I observe it at will, but I could have readily touched it, had I so desired. I called Sylvia, who helps me in the garden, and we marveled to our heart's content.

I thought about that, there in the early night, as birds twittered their last songs of the day, and peonies fragranced the coming darkness.

In my hand I held a little red book in which I record prayer requests. I had come to be with God, to seek His counsel on many matters, to lift my family and friends up in prayer, to plead for the Holy Spirit. But instead my heart was filled with praise. Praise must come first. Praise to a Creator God who did not choose to strip the earth of beauty when humanity sinned, but who left His signature of love everywhere upon this sad planet.

My gardens are created in His honor, a tribute to His divine imagination and His generosity in letting us tap into His creativity.

I know someday He'll return Eve to her garden, and as she walks familiar paths, touches familiar shrubs, sniffs familiar roses, and lifts her hand to a favorite bird, her heart will leap with gratitude toward a love that has more meaning than it had on the first morning of time. Hers and our praise, born of suffering and trial, will rise in an anthem such as the universe has never heard. Tonight, here on tarnished Planet Earth, I practice for that day.

I praise You, Lord, for what I now see and know, and all that is to come. Amen.

I sing for joy at the works of your hands (Ps. 92:4).

What Should I Have Done?

Lunch-hour traffic made our exit from the mall parking lot tedious and frustrating.

"We're going to be late getting Dad's sandwiches made if we don't catch a hole in this traffic pretty soon," daughter Amy said, impatiently nosing the car a bit closer to the main highway.

"We shouldn't have lingered so long in the stores," I berated myself.

"Look at that little old man!" I heard the amazement in Amy's voice even before my eyes found the short, aged figure beyond the wall of traffic. Though surely well into his 70s, he stood in the 90-degree heat, bent nearly double with a battered suitcase and a bedroll, yanking his thumb almost angrily at the passing cars.

Just then Amy whipped us out into a small gap in the traffic and asked simultaneously, "Shall we pick him up?" Now, we both knew the dangers of stopping for hitchhikers, but this human being, his weathered face scarlet in the intense sunlight, looked close to collapse. I hesitated, aware that an old man could ease a gun out of a suitcase just as efficiently as a young man, but it also seemed to me that he could easily die right there beside the road while we cautious motorists whizzed by. Even before I nodded assent, Amy was stopping. The cars piled up behind us as he loaded his gear into the back seat and climbed slowly in. We asked him where he was headed.

"Rochester. Came in on the bus from Buffalo this morning, but didn't have money to go on, so decided to thumb. It won't take me long. Can't be more than 35 miles, can it?" No defeat in his voice. Whatever had brought him to this place had not destroyed his pluck.

"It's just about 35 miles," I replied. "We won't be much help to you. We're going only a short distance. What are you going to do in Rochester? Do you have family there?"

He leaned forward in the seat, obviously straining to hear me. "No family. I'm looking for work. I hear Kodak and Bausch & Lomb are both there. Ought to find something easy."

Amy and I exchanged glances. In the present economy the application lines stretched long at both industries, and a man his age wouldn't stand a chance. As we approached the turnoff for our road, I knew I could never leave him there in the blazing sun without so much as a tree for shelter. Quietly I said to Amy, "Take us home. I'm going to drop you and the groceries off. You can fix Dad's lunch, and I'll drive our passenger back to town and put him on the bus for Rochester." When I shouted our plan to him over the back of the seat, he didn't argue.

As we turned into our circular driveway and he viewed the expanse of lawns and pond and orchards, he said, "You've got a right pretty place here." Somehow the cool green surroundings didn't look as good to me as usual.

On the way back to town we didn't talk, because I couldn't drive and make him hear at the same time, but I glanced at him occasionally in the rearview mirror. He had removed his old hat and laid his head back against the seat, eyes closed, relaxing in the air-conditioned comfort. His sweaty white hair clung to his forehead, and he looked terribly fragile. I thought of the grandfather I had once loved fiercely.

When I pulled up at the bus station, I handed him money, enough to get his ticket and buy a good meal. He thanked me with dignity.

At home my family razzed me a bit ("He probably laughed all the way to Rochester"; "He was probably a professional bum," etc.), but I knew they would all have done the same thing.

I cannot forget him. At night as I fall asleep, I wonder if, 35 miles away, he's rolled up in his ragged bedroll on a park bench with an empty stomach. My solution now seems so easy, so temporary, so useless.

What should I have done?

Whatever you did for one of the least of these brothers of mine, you did for me (Matt. 25:40).

Nobody's Child

This is Joe's story and probably the story of thousands of us who got off to a rough start.

Joe was born during the Depression, and his parents' marriage fell apart along with the economy. At 17 months he went to live in the home of his paternal grandparents. His mother, though struggling with problems of survival, tried to visit him frequently, bringing him clothes and little gifts.

Into his grandparents' home came a steady stream of uncles, aunts, and cousins. He felt the warmth of that close-knit Southern family, but he could never find his place in its glow. He saw fathers and sons go fishing and the maternal pride in childish accomplishments. Though he was treated kindly, even loved, he stood outside the circle—nobody's child.

His grandmother, though illiterate—unable to read even the Bible— knew and loved Jesus Christ. She'd raised, besides her own 10 children, two or three other needy youngsters. While his heart hungered for his mother, he saw in this godly woman a generosity of spirit, a concern for humanity, which shaped and altered his life.

There *were* times when one of the passing cars nosed down into his dusty lane and brought his mother. These high days stood out in the lad's lonely life. He clutched at the moments, cherishing her voice, memorizing her smile, blossoming beneath her touch. When she left, he pleaded to go with her, clinging to her and stabbing her reasonings with his tears. What did he care that meals were sure at his grandfather's table, that care was more constant? All he wanted was her presence. But always the visit ended—the car moved relentlessly down the lane until his mother's face became a blur and her waving hand a symbol of his ever-present sorrow. He raced behind the car, small tanned legs churning the Oklahoma dust, until at last the distance between them widened into hopelessness, his frantic cries of "Mother, Mother, take me with you!" ended.

Small wonder that at 18 he joined the Army and opened his arms wide to most of the enticements this world offers.

Joe's a preacher today, and he uses this story in one of his best sermons. He tells it absolutely dry-eyed while drawing the following conclusions.

1. It was his grandmother's early training that led him, some rough-and-tumble years later, back to Christ. Let this be encouragement to those grandmothers, foster mothers, even adoptive mothers, who can never quite find their way into the hearts of the wistful children under their care.

2. Out of Joe's childhood came a special compassion. Today he looks at the children in his congregation with empathy. He watches their home life, their heartbreaks, their needs, and their joys with tender concern, for he's been there.

3. In looking back, he sees that God was always there, caring, watching, waiting for him. "Since I have committed myself to Him," he affirms, "He's led me, with my wife and children, in a marvelous way."

It's a joyous footnote that his mother, long a stranger to Christ, now walks with him in the faith he loves.

I drew two conclusions from the story myself. Perhaps you'll have a couple of your own.

1. Children's need of their mother is so deep and consuming that they should never be denied it, except under the most extreme conditions.

2. Joe today is a gentle, calm, compassionate man. He carries no outward evidence of inner scars. His smile flashes quick and warm, and his eyes often dance merrily.

There's a gospel song that speaks of picking up the broken pieces of our lives and giving them to our Lord, who will put those pieces back together and make our lives complete.

That's what He did for Joe. So if your life has some broken pieces, don't use them for a crutch. Just ask God to start patching way back at the beginning, to help you let go of the hurts and bitterness that may yet twist and writhe within you. He'll turn what you endured into something lovely and useful . . . and give you His peace. Let me say He's done that for me also, and Joe and I can't both be wrong.

"But I will restore you to health and heal your wounds," declares the Lord (Jer. 30:17).

Places I've Lived and Hope to Live

I've always liked turning a house into a home. Had I ever been catapulted into the nomadic existence of today's upwardly mobile society, I would not have counted it a catastrophe. There's something about walking into a strange house, bereft of rugs, curtains, and furniture, that triggers all my decorating instincts. Limited funds only add to the challenge and send me off to flea markets and garage sales.

I guess it all started on the Vermont farm where I spent my childhood. Looking back on the decor of our farmhouse there in the 1930s, I have to smile. It was home, and it seemed the best spot on earth to me, but I fear it could well have been labeled "Early Depression." Somehow my grandmother's houseplants and the cheery warmth of wood stoves provided an illusion of coziness. Strangely, I did not long to redecorate that ancient New England house.

When I was about 9, however, the domestic urge came upon me. I scoured the attic, basement, garage, and barn for abandoned furniture, all of which I tugged up the hill that rose gently behind our house. In a sort of hollow on the hillside, shaded with small trees and shrubs, I set up housekeeping. There I could dine like a sultan in my leafy bower, with a long green valley sprawling beneath me.

Occasionally in the radiance of noonday I'd decide to spend the night in my "apartment," but when darkness closed in, usually the padding (imagined or otherwise) of four-footed creatures sent me dashing to a walled dwelling. (As an experienced berrypicker I was all too aware of bears and bobcats.)

Since then I have had opportunity to exercise my limited skills on various apartments and a house or two. We've lived in our present home for 30 years, and it has survived many a change of mind and decor. In the early years there weren't many options. Cheap and childproof were the criteria. It was just as well, for I hadn't learned much since furnishing my hillside bower. Only now, after years of experimenting, am I beginning to know exactly what I like and how to achieve it. At long last, with the children's college bills behind us, there's a bit more money for embellishing this old New York farmhouse.

My favorite area is a newly decorated bedroom with softly flowered lavender paper below the chair rail and a simple off-white with small lavender flowers above. There's an Abigail Adams bedspread on the four-poster and heavily ruffled swags at the windows. An old tin pail overflows with dried larkspur and German statice. I've chosen not to cover the pine floor, which has mellowed to a warm gold.

Someday, I'm well aware, my lovely lavender room will be no more. This pleasant farm will become but rubble (Rev. 16:17-20). Therefore, it behooves me not to set my heart on pine floors and stone fireplaces, however much they may gladden our present existence.

I understand a home is being prepared for me elsewhere, something quite beyond my present abode (John 14:1-3; Rev. 21). I am not at all sure my meager decorating talents will be equal to this magnificent dwelling, but somehow that doesn't concern me.

(On Planet Earth our homes are a refuge in a stormy, often unsafe environment. We make them cozy and welcoming to ease our loneliness, cut off as we are from our original carefree and exotic surroundings and their Creator (Gen. 2:8, 9). When the problem of our lostness is solved, however, and we bask once more in the glory of God, we won't need the pallid comfort of favorite paintings and early American furniture. The sweet peace of heaven will infiltrate our beings, and instead of moving inward, gathering about hearths, we will wing our way outward into a vast universe that invites fearless exploration, one where all is harmony with divine law. May you and I let nothing stand between us and that ultimate home.)

In my Father's house are many rooms. . . . I am going there to prepare a place for you (John 14:2).

For Breadmakers—and Others

Last Mother's Day our son Mitch and his wife gave me a DAK breadmaker. I used to make bread regularly, but as my writing/speaking career progressed, some of my housewifely arts fell, of necessity, by the wayside, breadmaking among them.

Surely, thought Mitch, I'd have time for this magical machine, and he was right. I do. I simply dump all the ingredients for one loaf into the container, close its glass dome and push a button. So amazing is it to watch the process that it's a great temptation to waste all the saved time by observing the bread mix, knead, rise, and bake—all by itself.

Somehow, in the past, women who knew how to bake bread always had a little edge over those who didn't, but watching this machine whiz through the process is very humbling. Alas, the mystery is gone. But the bread is delicious!

So much was homemade bread a part of my childhood that I grew up thinking a loaf of fluffy white store bread was a great treat. A large barrel of flour always sat to the right of the kneading board in our pantry, and yeast, wrapped in shiny paper, came in small cubes. Three times a week the wonderful aroma of baking bread filled the house, and anyone around, when it came out of the oven, was free to slice off a crust and slather it with homemade butter. (This was only a fraction of each week's baking extravaganza. From that same oven rolled pies, cakes, cookies, rolls, muffins. Small wonder that people formed terrible eating habits and died young!)

One time when a large pan of bread (six or eight loaves worth) was rising, high on the back of the wood stove, a relative stopped by and invited my grandmother (in whose home I lived) and me to go berrypicking. Thinking we would not be gone long, Grandma accepted.

We found a glorious berry patch where the fruit could be picked by the handfuls. As we greedily filled our pails, all thought of the rising bread was erased from our minds.

When we finally walked into the kitchen, several hours later, great mounds of dough hung from the warming oven like clouds on a summer day. My great-aunt and I bent double with laughter, but Grandma wasn't so sure it was funny. Preparing that amount of dough was both toilsome and time-consuming. Finally, having a good sense of humor, she couldn't help seeing the amusing side of it and joined us in our fits of giggling.

Bread, of one type or another, has long been a staple of humanity's diet. The first breads were hard and flat, consisting of only two ingredients, ground grain and water. This mixture was baked in the sun on hot rocks. While it doesn't sound too appetizing, it could well have been more healthful than the bleached, preservative-ridden loaves we eat today.

The first records of leavened bread are found in Egyptian culture. The soft, light loaves were a pleasant change from previous plain fare. Ovens became the solution to the need for an enclosed heated area in which to bake these larger masses of dough thoroughly.

In the early 1900s about 95 percent of all bread was baked at home. Fifty years later 95 percent of all bread was baked in bakeries and purchased by the consumer.

But bread never loses its popularity. Toast for breakfast, sandwiches for lunch, rolls for dinner. And today we have cosmopolitan taste buds . . . French bread, tortillas, pitas, Jewish rye, etc.

So when Jesus said, "I am the Bread of Life," He was making a plain but profound statement that would speak to every generation. We can get along without cupcakes and casseroles. If poverty were to strike, I would spend a good portion of our scanty food budget on healthful ingredients for bread, knowing its nutritional value. I think Jesus is telling us He is the essential element in our lives, as bread is in our diet. In *The Desire of Ages* the author says, of the unbelieving people of Christ's day, "Had they understood the Scriptures, they would have understood His words when He said, 'I am the bread of life!' " (p. 386).

So if you and I wish to comprehend that simple statement at its deepest levels, we must open the Bible. Study His feeding of the 5,000, His gift of manna to Israel, and the significance of the Communion bread. "I am the living bread that came down from heaven: if anyone eats of this bread he will live forever" (John 6:51).

I am the bread of life. He who comes to me will never go hungry (John 6:35).

The Message in the Bottle

While browsing in a Hallmark shop, I came upon a card that, for some reason, startled me. Even though I moved away from it to explore the get-well section, I kept coming back. I don't know what it said inside. I'm not sure I even looked, so fascinated was I with its exterior.

It was a simple painting of an expanse of ocean on which bobbed the legendary corked bottle. You know, the one bearing a message. Except this message was not in script, nor was it signed. Instead, inside the bottle flourished a miniature paradise. Tiny palm trees lent their shade to bright tropical flowers, while fountains shattered sunlight into jeweled spray. Exotic birds flitted among the shrubbery.

That scene spoke forcefully to something inside me. It was a message, but not a clear one. It danced tantalizingly upon the circumference of my mind, refusing to enter for my scrutiny. I showed it to my daughter, but she gave me a look that hinted both the card and I were a bit daffy. No decoding to be gained there.

The little scene is etched forever upon my memory. What did the artist have in mind? After days of intermittent pondering, I decided we all want paradise in a bottle. We'd love to find it cast up on some sandy shore or at least floating safely within wading distance.

Eden was once ours—serene, lush, and free of death, disease, and crime. Through a tragic rejection of divine counsel, its gates closed forever to us. We've been looking for Edens ever since. The problem is we are no longer fit inhabitants for Eden, though we like to think otherwise. We optimistically picture ourselves drifting off to eternal bliss, at our death, without much honest evaluation of our readiness.

We want an Eden free of crime—and it's true most of us aren't thieves, murderers, or rapists—but are we ready to abandon the gossip, white lies, and caustic retorts with which we assault the sensitive hearts of our fellow humans?

We want glowing health, but are we really ready for a lifestyle bereft of fats, sugars, and tobacco? Or do we want health and all the lethal goodies too?

We want a pure land, but would our frivolous speech and off-color jokes fall crudely in a holy environment?

Do we seek an Eden where the starving no longer flicker across our television screens, where the poor are tended neatly behind the scenes, with no annoying pleas to our pocketbooks?

Perhaps we hope to soak up all the benefits of paradise without becoming too involved personally, but you see, of course, it would never work. For unless each inhabitant had that original beauty of character, all the flamingos in the world would do no good. Eden is not so much a *place* as a *perspective*. Are we ready to change our perspective, or do we rather like this old world with its easygoing morals and undisciplined lifestyle? Maybe we'd just prefer to move it all to a Hawaiian setting and let sin have its pleasant way. (There would still be the small matters of cancer, battered wives, crippled children, alcoholics, etc., but we've lived with them a long time. We can keep doing so if they don't come too close.)

Was that the message in the bottle? Was it a warning for us all that Edens are not so easily come by?

I suspect only He who made that early garden with its guileless inhabitants can bring us around full circle. Only He can re-create the desire for holiness that we lack. Only He can put a new heart (with a distaste for evil) into these sin-addicted frames of ours. Then, and only then, will we regain our Eden.

Let us fall to our knees.

If anyone would come after me, he must deny himself and take up his cross and follow me. For whoever wants to save his life will lose it, but whoever loses his life for me will find it (Matt. 16:24, 25).

What My Bible Means to Me

Moments come when I don't want any part of the Bible. Sometimes when I pick it up to study, there's a curious rebellion within me. But I have gradually come to recognize this sensation as the devil running scared. For he is frightened, you know, when he sees us open the Book. He well knows it sings and sparks of another way of life, now closed to him, but still open to us. He's skilled at thought suggestion, and there have been times when I actually fell for his "You have no time for nonessentials today," or "It's pretty heavy reading—how about the new *McCalls?*" or "You'd be better off visiting your friend in the nursing home than sitting around reading."

Usually these days, however, I ignore his promptings, but even as I begin to read, sometimes that curious reluctance lingers. The trick, again, is to ignore it. Then, slowly, I am caught up in that other world of which I read. For it *is* another world, whether one in wandering with Abraham or pondering the new lifestyle of a converted Paul. A world in which men and women are reaching out fearfully, hopefully, toward that Being from whom they sprang, to whom they belong, and for whom they are ever lonely.

It's a story of failure and despair, forgiveness and hope, and always the love and concern of God hovering over His wayward planet. (Any parent who's ever watched a loved child head down all the wrong paths knows the feeling.)

But the Bible is even more than an account of our long struggle to find the way back to Eden. It is a personal letter to *me* from *my* God, and such is the magic of the Book that it is also an individual message to you as well. It will speak to your particular personality and hang-ups just as specifically as it does to mine. Only God could offer a Book so grand and general in theme, yet so personally and uniquely slanted to each human being.

My Bible is rather like a journal of the past 45 years of my life. (I didn't study it seriously before that.) As I browse here and there, I remember when this verse, or that, came sharply into focus, usually out of my own momentary predicament.

As a tearful young woman whose husband had just been borrowed by Uncle Sam, I stumbled onto Job 23:10: "He knows the way that I take; when he has tested me, I will come forth as gold." That verse sustained me through a loneliness that approached physical illness. It may be just empty words to one who's never needed it.

Beside Psalm 37:24 is penned the following: "The most encouraging words I ever read—8/6/68." I no longer even remember the reason it was so important to me on that particular date, but the message has stayed with me. "If the Lord delights in a man's way, he makes his steps firm; though he stumble, he will not fall, for the Lord upholds him with his hand." As the mother of six, I well knew the feeling of catching, before knee and pavement made contact, a little one who had stumbled. I had learned to keep a good firm grip on small hands. It wasn't hard at all for me to picture myself as the "toe-stubber" and God as the "picker-upper." A promise for today when all is well and for tomorrow when all may not be well. I think I shall make a necklace of such promises, and when I'm in a dull situation, I shall dwell upon them, as some ladies toy with their pearls.

Perhaps my Bible means most of all to me on Sabbath mornings when I rise early and go to my prayer garden at the south end of our big red barn. There, on a little terrace, with the fountain tinkling in the sun, the day still fresh and cool, I open the Bible with anticipation—lately to the Gospel of John. Verse by verse I explore John's view of Jesus Christ. All about me the earth offers apple blossoms and swallow ballets as evidence of His love and creativity. Somehow His words to me and His gift of beauty all combine with my own adoration for Him to make for a total experience. Most experiences today are a bit frayed at the edges. The breakfast hour and the demands of my family beckon, but I am reluctant to leave, for there in that sacred spot, His words are ever new and life-changing.

I'm sorry, Satan, but I want that life you chose to scorn, and the more I read my ragged old Bible, the more I want it.

I have hidden your word in my heart that I might not sin against you (Ps. 119:11).

Transparent as Sunlight

Long ago in the hills of Vermont I had a little friend named Winona, who lived two miles beyond my home along our country road. We often walked to meet each other and sat on a narrow bridge above a mountain stream, dangling our feet in the cool water and indulging in 9-year-old chatter. Each spring we shared a splendid secret. We knew where the trailing arbutus grew. Since the flower was rare and protected even then, one had to prowl the woods like an Indian scout to find a blossom or two. But ours was a patch, a tiny island of pink, tucked in the lee of a rock.

Awed by the laws protecting it, we would not have dreamed of picking a single stem, but we liked to lie on our bellies, chins in hands, admiring our discovery. We always worried it would somehow disappear during the fierce winter, as wildflowers are prone to do. We marveled that we alone enjoyed its dainty display.

"If we didn't come to look," Winona would say, "it would bloom and fade without a single eye to appreciate it."

And she was right. No one wandered in those endless forests except two little girls with time on their hands.

It was my first awareness of beauty with no particular purpose.

Many years later, our youngest son, when living in southern

California, took us up into the San Bernardino Mountains, and, to my astonishment, wild lupines and irises bloomed along our path. In fact, small sunlit clearings looked almost like cultivated gardens, so artistically were the flowers arranged by their divine Landscaper. I echoed Winona's wonder out of the long past. "I can't believe these flowers grow here year after year, far from the dwellings of human beings." It was a treasured day I shall never forget.

Again I was impressed with the fact that God scatters loveliness indiscriminately. Rare and exotic birds dart about in inaccessible places, and sunlight dapples cool, shady corridors untrampled by human feet.

That insight into God's character, His consistent concern for loveliness and order everywhere, seen or unseen, suddenly translated into very practical messages for me. I began to delight in this idea of hidden beauty. It meant my cupboards and closets should be as tidy as my living room, my around-the-house clothes as attractive as my downtown clothes, my secluded garden as weed-free as the one seen from the highway.

But more than that, it meant that my private acts should be as moral and kind as my public ones, my words spoken in the home as gentle as those in the marketplace or at church. If this principle were carried into every corner of my life, the results would be staggering.

A wise and dedicated lady once wrote: "Everything that Christians do should be as transparent as the sunlight." I liked that so much I had it copied in calligraphy and framed for my office. I long to experience such purity of character, to become a participating member of God's orderly universe, where beauty flourishes in the most unexpected corners and in the most unexpected hearts. Will you join me?

For there is nothing hidden that will not be disclosed, and nothing concealed that will not be known or brought out into the open (Luke 8:17).

Smoke Bush Surgery

Today as I checked one of my gardens, I noted that the smoke bush (*Cotinus coggygria* "purpureus") was unusually lovely. Elegant deep purple leaves cloaked its perfectly rounded form, and over the leaves the soft haze of its fruiting panicles rose, indeed, like a purple smoke. At its best, it's a unique and breathtaking shrub. I can never refrain from touching its airy exterior.

It has had seasons when it was not as pleasing to the eye, especially its first. Initially, though small, it prospered and even sent out a few puffs of its proverbial "smoke." But by midsummer an entire section began to wilt, then grow brown and crisp. I do not have a lot of patience with finicky plants, and was about to discard it.

It was Sylvia who intervened. Sylvia is a young woman who makes my love affair with gardens possible. Though I spend as many hours as possible planting, weeding, and pruning, my time is limited, and it's Sylvia who does many of the tasks that extensive gardens require.

So she it was who, noting the feeble condition of the smoke bush, gave it a generous dose of TLC. First she dug about it, watered it, trimmed off the ailing stems, and waited, hopefully, for it to recover. But instead another section began to wither.

At this point I would surely have tugged it out and tossed it on the trash pile, but I was too polite to meddle with Sylvia's patient. I was also curious to see how far she would go in her rescue mission.

One day she came into the house carrying a long, thick, contorted root, an odd-looking specimen. "That's what was strangling our poor smoke bush," she said, obviously as excited as any surgeon after a successful session.

"What is it?" I asked, touching the rather ugly and otherworldly object in her hand.

"I have no idea. It didn't appear to have any top, but it was certainly vicious underground. It had snarled itself so tightly about the root of the smoke bush that it was literally choking the plant."

From that point on, the shrub, free of its deadly foe, flourished. I never look at it without being reminded that it owes its life to my young helper, who had pity for even an ailing plant, and the patience to try again. (It's not the only horticultural lesson she's taught me, and I'm supposed to be the gardener!)

The smoke bush always reminds me of how God moves right in when we begin to wither spiritually and goes straight to the heart of the problem. Unlike the rosy shrub, however, we sometimes reject the treatment or withdraw because it's painful.

I'm so thankful that God, like Sylvia, perseveres. I'm learning to pray "Lord, deliver me from the root that strangles, no matter how much I rebel and complain, that I might develop to my full potential in Christ, reflecting His character, to His glory."

Search me, O God, and know my heart; test me and know my anxious thoughts. See if there is any offensive way in me, and lead me in the way everlasting (Ps. 139:23, 24).

Namesake

W e're awaiting a phone call announcing the arrival of our fourth grandchild. This morning our son-in-law called saying that Lori, our Korean daughter, had gone into the hospital for the birth of her first child.

She wants a little girl to name Mindy June. Since I've never had a namesake, I secretly hope for a girl myself, but the father-to-be wants a son. So however it turns out, someone will be especially happy, and we will all rejoice, for a new life, whatever its gender, is reason for celebration.

As the day creeps along, I will Lori strength for the painful process and send up many a prayer for her safety.

I think of her own sad, war-shattered beginning, of which we know so little. She came to us at 2, a pathetic, cautious little waif with eyes that had seen too much. She was not afraid. She was past fear, simply existing in a world of hunger, sorrow, and abuse.

She ate ravenously whatever we set before her. Survival was still high on her list of priorities. A very good sign. In time—quite a lot of time—she crinkled up her pretty little face and laughed. Whatever had been her lot in those first two years, it had not totally destroyed her faith in the human race. Slowly she allowed herself to trust, to love, and—to a degree—to respond. But there were scars. A tendency to depression. A painful shyness. An inability to verbalize her deepest emotions.

Marriage had been a blessing. Her husband's pride in her delicate Oriental beauty was a splendid tonic for her self-esteem.

And now she was to hold her offspring in her arms. A little one with its American blood lines mixed with a heritage reaching far back into the proud, pure race of Korea. For our Lori, it could not help being a high moment. It would be the first blood relative she had ever seen. She had adopted relatives and in-laws, but this small new creature would be a blood relative.

It's interesting to think of God breathing into Adam the breath of life. Surely that made humans kin with divinity in a very special way.

But breath is not blood.

I used to think of Christians as adopted into the heavenly community through the merits of Christ. Our family knows a lot about adoption. We've seen it function right along beside blood relationships and work very efficiently, but the adoptees would tell you that, even under the best of circumstances, something is missing. That's why Lori will know a special joy when she holds her infant for the first time.

It occurred to me recently, however, that Jesus voluntarily made Himself our blood relative. He broke from Mary's womb with the blood of humanity surging in His veins. Later He spilled that same human blood on a rock called Calvary, in an act that made us more than blood relatives.

We have no earthly relationships with which to compare this experience. Oh, humans have, on occasion, died for each other. But there were issues at stake on Golgotha beyond our puny comprehension. He took on, and then shed, our human blood at the risk of losing a Father-Son relationship the like of which we know nothing.

In the light of all this, human concern over birth and adoption pales. We are all brothers and sisters in Christ and, beyond that, grafted into the divine relationship that we grasp but dimly now, but that will astonish and delight us eternally with its intensity.

The phone rings. I pick it up eagerly. I am grandmother of a 5-pound 12-ounce boy. So much for namesakes. Welcome to earth, Vincent Mitchell Sands.

For you know that it was not with perishable things such as silver or gold that you were redeemed . . . , but with the precious blood of Christ, a lamb without blemish or defect (1 Peter 1:18, 19).

Uprooting

September is my favorite month, with May and October running a close second and third. No matter how busy I am, I spend time outdoors in these special periods. Somehow September retains the best of summer even while easing us into the rigors of fall. Flowers bloom generously once more as though they too enjoy this drowsy interim of warm days and cool nights.

This morning, as I took my walk around our "back forty," a tall white pine, glistening in sunlight, caught my attention. Nothing picks up light quite like the long graceful needles of the white pine. As I stood, head back, admiring its beauty, I thought of the day years ago we brought it from New Hampshire. There, hiking behind a relative's home, Don and I came upon a monstrous white pine, a real specimen. We circled around its broad base, viewing it from every angle. It was flawless.

But, of course, one does not move a 40-foot evergreen. However—aha—at its base grew dozens of seedlings of various heights! Returning later with the proper tools and a bushel basket, we removed the finest of the lot. Now it towers over me here behind our New York home.

It isn't the tree its mother was. Evergreens don't really thrive in our too-fertile loam. They prefer the thin, well-drained, rocky soil of New England pastures. But it has struggled to a good height in spite of its removal to a foreign environment.

I, too, was once uprooted. After five years of dormitory life, marriage transplanted me from New England to New York State. You see why I empathize with the tree. Though I had a handsome and caring young husband, I was lonely. The church was small, and we had few Christian friends our own age. There was a period in which I didn't much care whether my roots accepted the soil or not. But God tended that uprooting with the infinite care of a master gardener.

He knew I'd lived long enough in the flighty environment of campus levity. I needed to be alone. To be still. To think. To learn of Him. Whether I liked it or not. In time, I did all those things, to my eternal benefit. I even came to thank the Uprooter for His divine understanding of my deepest needs.

Now that I think about it, some very important biblical figures experienced painful transplantings.

Joseph, uprooted from his shepherd's home and sold into Egyptian slavery, became the deliverer of thousands.

Moses, torn from his childhood home at an early age to take his place as an adopted son in the royal palace, also became a mighty deliverer.

Daniel, marched as a Babylonian prisoner across burning deserts, rose to power in a hostile land because His relationship with the Gardener remained constant.

I guess my favorite uprooting story is that of the little Jewish captive who served her abductors so cheerfully and well that her master accepted her counsel to return to the prophet of Israel for healing of his leprosy (see 2 Kings 5). With what exquisite courage that little lass sank her roots into enemy territory!

We never know, you and I, at what moment we will be uprooted. Sometimes the uprootings are emotional rather than geographic. But let us remember that the Gardener is omnipresent and that He tends the fragile transplant with uncommon care.

For I am the Lord, your God, who takes hold of your right hand and says to you, Do not fear; I will help you (Isa. 41:13).

Optical Magic

Tonight my husband, Don, brought home something very strange and a bit heart-stopping. A coworker had given him a letter-sized sheet of paper on which a faintly recognizable image of Christ's face was printed. It was not appealing because, like a negative, the blacks and whites were reversed. He told me to stare at four tiny dots along the nose for 30 seconds, then to look immediately at the wall. I complied, having no idea what to expect. On the wall, before my astonished eyes, appeared a lovely black-and-white picture of Jesus (the reverse, of course, of the image at which I had been staring).

For me, it was startling, moving, and almost miraculous. The face upon the wall soon faded, but by blinking my eyes, I could recall it a time or two. I wanted to repeat the experience over and over. About then our daughter and her husband walked in, and I couldn't wait to have them try it. Even Amy, who is quite unflappable like her father, let out a reverent "Wow!" of astonishment as the face materialized. Brian found he had to blink to make it work for him.

About now, some of you who have not seen this optical phenomenon may be saying there's some unsavory hocus-pocus going on here, and I admit to accusing Don of bringing the occult into the house, but the truth is it has something to do with the retina of the eye and is quite explainable. Perhaps it has been around a long time and you're all smiling at my naïveté but no matter how many times I repeat the experience, the same sense of reverence and love comes over me. It's like a mini Second Coming, and I have to fight back tears. I guess you'd have to experience it to understand, and perhaps it doesn't affect others in the same way anyhow.

There is something about the Face on the wall, blurry as it is, that is both kind and compelling. It gets beyond my mind, beyond astonishment, and does something unfamiliar to my heart. It has made me realize that seeing Jesus at His coming will not send us into ecstatic celebration, but rather to our knees, weeping, in the deepest humility and gratitude.

I've often heard that seeing Jesus should be the ultimate goal of our pilgrimage heavenward. In my secret heart I've sometimes wondered if I would meet that standard, or would my eyes rove curiously to the 12 gates, the awesome beauty of the angels, the golden streets, and the shining sea of glass. But, somehow, as that hazy picture of Christ appears on the kitchen wall, I know, without the slightest doubt, that being near Him will be all that matters. I shall view the wonders of heaven eagerly, for even in this world, beauty has brought me tremendous comfort and happiness, but I don't think I'll ever want to leave the range of those loving eyes.

Just for a moment imagine Jesus calling out to you by name, and you turn and He's smiling, and in those eyes is more love than you've ever experienced from parent, spouse, child, or all three put together. You could undoubtedly throw in your best friend too. I like to think about it. It makes the day-to-day struggle here much less stressful.

Recently some friends of ours, two young couples, traveled to a remote vacation spot in Canada. For four hours they bumped over a crude road at low speed to arrive at the lodge. There they loaded all their supplies into a motorboat and traveled another half hour to their cabin on the long lake. It was a wearying journey, requiring patience, but the beauty and solitude they enjoyed for a week made the abuse of their vehicles and bones all worthwhile.

When they returned, it wasn't the bumps they talked about, but the nights of absolute quiet with only the howling of wolves to break the dark silence, the glassy calm of the lake, the camaraderie they shared. The bumps were forgotten.

That's how it will be when the Prince of the universe takes us home. Just walking beside Him will be enough, hearing His voice, knowing

He's aware of each one of us as though there were no other. All the bumps will be forgotten.

In your unfailing love you will lead the people you have redeemed (Ex. 15:13).

The Rocker That Went to College

Some years ago our youngest son left for college with an old rocking chair packed into the back seat of his car. He really didn't have room for it (at that point, even a toothbrush would have been an intrusion), but he'd become pretty well acquainted with the old chair over the summer, and he wasn't leaving it behind.

For a piece of nondescript furniture it had quite a history. I'd bought it years before at an auction for 75 cents. Obviously it was no antique, nor was it a thing of beauty. But it was solid and comfortable, and I'd had babies to rock. With a good high headrest and a firm back support, it felt just right for a tall person. Many a night the old chair and I watched the moon melt into dawn while an ill or sleepless toddler in my arms wrestled with insomnia. Somewhere along the way it acquired a coat of green paint to blend, as imperceptibly as possible, into one decor or another.

Eventually there came into our home a youngster from Korea—a lad who liked action. Often the old chair found itself operating at a pretty brisk pace. One day the inevitable happened. Chair and boy went end over teakettle. Boy unhurt. Family greatly amused. Chair minus its fine high headrest.

It broke so raggedly that repair seemed impossible, so the jagged ends were neatly sawed off, the headrest discarded, and the wounded chair carted off to a dark storage area in the barn. It could have been the end of the 75-cent chair, but old rockers don't give up that easily.

Fifteen years or more passed, and our youngest daughter took a year of school by correspondence. Optimistically she planned to finish in May, but the summer found her still bent over schoolbooks, so off she went to the barn for the old green chair, which she planted on our small front portico. If study she must, she'd absorb some summertime while she was working at it. "It's still comfortable, even without a headrest," she hollered through the screen door.

So once more the rocker found itself back in service. Because we didn't set great value upon it, no one bothered to bring it in when it rained, and the paint began to peel and curl. When Amy went off to boarding school that fall, I toted the shabby old relic back to the barn. And there it stayed until son Mitch, on cleaning the barn, spied it in its cobwebby retirement.

The peeling paint challenged him. He'd restore it—right down to the original wood. And he stuck to the project with amazing tenacity for one who did not like painstaking procedures. When the last coat of Min-Wax stain and sealer had been applied, it looked quite respectable. Our son knew every rung and groove more intimately than he had ever anticipated, so there was no question about squeezing it into the car. It had to go.

As he drove away, the rockers reared up in the back window like two horns, and I had myself a little chuckle. Momentarily, for me, the piece of furniture took on almost human qualities. No one had asked the old girl whether she wanted to come out of retirement and go off to college to become the soother of two budding pilots and their friends. How would she accept the shirts and jackets that would surely be draped over her crippled back? and the noise? and the wrestling? I had the feeling she'd take it all in easy stride.

I was being ridiculous, of course—playing games to cover the emptiness every mother feels when sons and daughters drive away to the ivy halls of learning. But I hoped I'd given, in my own sphere, the kind of patient, willing service the old rocker had contributed to our family. I asked myself some questions:

Was I dealing cheerfully with the physical and emotional wounds life had dealt? (Gave myself about a C− on that one. I do a lot of complaining about the ordinary ups and downs of life.)

Was I open, even eager, for new areas of service, no matter how far they might lead into unfamiliar territory? (Sometimes I swear I'll never accept another invitation to speak, because I hate leaving home.)

Could I endure, after I had given faithful service, the paint-peeling periods of life when no one took me seriously or was concerned about my welfare? (I wasn't sure.)

No more questions. The old rocker had shown me too much about myself already.

Lord, make me a faithful, uncomplaining servant to those who need me . . . anytime . . . anywhere.

Serve one another in love. . . . Carry each other's burdens, and in this way you will fulfill the law of Christ (Gal. 5:13-6:2).

Of Plaques and Peace

I always enter the large Christian bookstore in our area with an overwhelming sense of anticipation. Besides hundreds of enticing books and dozens of Bibles in every conceivable version, it carries lovely greeting cards and stationery, all witnessing to the Christian faith in tasteful ways. I seldom get away without an armful of purchases.

My favorite section of the store I save until last. Along the entire back wall hang plaques, large and small, most of them of stained and antiqued wood, appropriate for our century-old house. One, in a lovely slate blue, has a background painting of a cozy room, beneath which is printed:

> "Only one life,
> 'Twill soon be past.
> Only what's done for
> Christ will last."

Another plaque features a primitive farm scene, with stiff little cows on hillsides that roll to the horizon under puffy white clouds. It says:

> "Lord, bless our house as we come and go;
> Bless our home as the children grow.
> Bless our farms as we gather in;
> Lord, bless us all with love and friends."

Though I've scrutinized these artistic wall hangings many times, I've never purchased one. While they are a bit expensive, there's another reason for my reluctance. Once I did buy a small inexpensive plaque, not for its beauty but for its message: "Lord, let my life be a reflection of my love for You." I thought *If I hang this in the kitchen where I will see it a hundred times a day, it will inspire me to live a pure and beautiful life.*

At first I read it many times a day and was challenged to do well. But gradually I ceased to see it anymore. It became as common and unnoticed as the spatulas and salad molds hanging from hooks about the kitchen.

That experience taught me two things. First, no saying, however direct and penetrating, will have a permanent, life-changing effect. Second, no matter how many religious wall hangings one has indicating that "Christ is the head of this house" (or whatever), the guest will read one's lifestyle far more readily and absorb its message.

A young woman who married into an Adventist family told me recently, "I was amazed at Eric's home when I first began to visit there.

I felt a peace when I entered. His parents always spoke calmly and pleasantly to each other. They had a closeness and love, a kind of holy presence in their home."

As she spoke I thought of the plaques at the bookstore. How foolish they seemed beside such a testimony! When the spirit of Christ lives in our home, we need no plaques.

A dear friend, not of our faith, who was experiencing heartbreaking marital problems called on a Friday night to ask if she might come talk with me the next morning. She said, "I know you go to church, but could I come early? I need you so desperately." We arranged for her to come at 6:00, since I knew my family would be sleeping at that hour and we would have privacy.

The morning dawned windy and snowy, so I built a fire and pulled two chairs close to the hearth before she came chugging up the driveway in her little VW. We talked and prayed and shed a few tears before my household came to life a couple of hours later. I invited her to stay for breakfast, which she did.

It all seemed very routine to me, but later she wrote, "There was something in your house, a sweet peace. Your children were lively and happy, but I sensed the Sabbath sacredness so strongly it was almost tangible." I hope that taste of Sabbath joy will lodge in her memory for later decision-making.

Plaques are fine, but what we really need are lives that so reflect Jesus that our neighbors and friends will hunger to be enfolded in that aura of peace and love. Then we can share with them its Source.

Live such good lives among the pagans that, though they accuse you of doing wrong, they may see your good deeds and glorify God on the day he visits us (1 Peter 2:12).

Children of Sorrow and Grief

I opened the letter with interest. Though a writer often receives hundreds of letters, for me the fascination never wanes. Someone out there has taken the time to make contact, and I'm both curious and grateful. The picture I held in my hand stirred some memory out of the past. The face . . . so familiar.

It took a few moments for my brain to sort out the schoolmates of 40 years ago, but finally I was able to put a name with the face. She had read my books and felt moved to renew our acquaintance.

I'll call her Marla. She and her sister had arrived on our campus at midyear. Bright and pretty, they made quite a splash. We girls assessed them a bit too attractive and a very real threat to our carefully tended relationships with the occupants of the boys' dorm on the other side of the campus.

As I read the letter in my hand, my vision blurred.

"When I knew you in college, my heart went out to you because I heard you too were an orphan. [I wasn't technically an orphan, though I'd been thoroughly stripped of mothers and mother substitutes.]

"Barbara and I had been waifs in a foundling home and during our teens often felt a desperate loneliness for our own mother in whom to confide. We yearned for her love and understanding through those years."

I looked at the picture through new eyes. We'd had so much in common, and I'd never known.

She'd seemed so strong, so sure of herself, in those far-off days. How well I now understood the hardy exterior she'd developed as a shell against a world that never seemed to play quite fair.

"When I was 3," the letter went on, "my mother visited us at the orphanage. I remember she hugged and kissed us, and then, taking a small mirror from her purse, showed us the lipstick imprint of her kiss upon our cheeks. A year later she took her own life."

I wept for those girls and for thousands like them who've been mothered by sorrow and fathered by grief. What do such experiences do to a child? Because I've had in my own home the children of war and trauma, I can answer with some assurance.

The hardy children grow tougher, often rejecting their own tenderness and vulnerability lest they be overpowered by pain. They achieve, driving themselves on and on, to prove they were, after all, of value.

The sensitive, weaker children retreat from life, accepting no challenges. They cling to people pathetically. They're fragile and helpless and back off whenever the going gets tough. They have no stamina and cannot make decisions.

Sad, you say. Indeed. But let me share with you the closing lines from Marla's letter.

"We often marvel, Barb and I, that we've become decent adults and parents. And we praise God for His watchcare over us, and for His patient love. Isn't Jesus wonderful!"

So the sad picture is suddenly aglow with a shaft of sunlight. Jesus enters the gloom, touches the torn and tattered lives, and somehow uses the heartbreak to re-create unusually tender and compassionate men and women. Out of the broken threads, Christ, the Mender, spins lovely lives.

So if you were born to tears, weep no more, lest you miss Him when He passes by and calls to you. "His compassions never fail. They are new every morning" (Lam. 3:22, 23).

And my God will meet all your needs according to his glorious riches in Christ Jesus (Phil. 4:19).

He Is Able

Joshua 10:25 was highlighted very visibly for me by the Holy Spirit about 15 years ago. (If you don't believe the Holy Spirit does that, then you have yet to make an exciting discovery, and should read John Sherrill's book *My Friend, the Bible.*) I had experienced many times the wonder of a text blazing into my present condition as fresh as sunrise. No matter that it had been written a few thousand years ago. That's the magic of God's Word.

So when this particular verse, as I was reading Joshua 10, leaped out from the page, I took note. John Sherrill calls it a "stopping verse." I reread it. Again. Again.

Actually, it's part of a most unsavory story. One of those Old Testament stories that makes a point, but is a bit too violent and bloody for my taste. The event followed that high day in Israel when the sun stood still and God fought for His people. It seems five scared kings had holed up in a cave. Eventually Joshua had them brought out and the captains of war placed their feet upon the kings' bowed necks. Then Joshua "slew them and hanged them on five trees: and they were hanging upon the trees until the evening" (Joshua 10:26).

At the point where Israelite warriors had their feet upon the necks of heathen royalty, Joshua made his proclamation: "Thus shall the Lord do to all your enemies against whom ye fight" (verse 25, KJV). Great assurance for Israel, or at least it should have been.

In 1978 when I read the account, I was struggling with the problem of sin. At the time of conversion, in my early 20s, I had made right all the ugly errors of my past that I could recall. It was a humbling experience. I didn't have any addictive vices (at least that I recognized

70

as such) with which to do battle, so there came a moment when I felt clean and spiritually invigorated. But as I journeyed on with Christ, He began gently to point out some areas in which all was not well. Subtle sins. As I held myself up to the standard set in the Bible, especially by Christ, I realized the war had only begun.

I began to attack these defects of character with willpower, thinking my disciplined New England genes would make short work of them. After some years of failure, I conceded that there were evils which simply would not yield to determination.

Somewhere during this time Morris Venden came on the scene with his version of righteousness by faith. I began to comprehend dimly that the only way any of us sinners were ever going to fit into the heavenly community was to admit our failure to gain the victory (another humbling step) and back off so God could do it for us. (The term *God* in this context involves our triune God.)

I grew very discouraged in this long process. Nothing moved quickly enough to suit me. (If God was so willing to deliver, where was He? These sins were becoming more offensive to me each day.) One text was a great comfort and encouragement during this bleak time:

"I pray also that the eyes of your heart may be enlightened in order that you may know the hope to which he has called you, the riches of his glorious inheritance in the saints, *and his incomparably great power for us who believe. That power is like the working of his mighty strength, which he exerted in Christ when he raised him from the dead*" (Eph. 1:18-20).

That verse assured me there was plenty of power. I surely needed to be raised from spiritual death, and God was able. Why wasn't He willing? Why wasn't that "incomparable power" working for me?

Later another text shed light upon my problem:

"When the Lord heard them, he was very angry; his fire broke out against Jacob, and his wrath rose against Israel, *for they did not believe in God or trust in his deliverance* (Ps. 78:21, 22).

Was lack of faith my problem? As the years slipped by, it had grown pretty shaky. Was my eternal fretting barring the door to God's deliverance?

It was Joshua 10:25, however, that finally opened my eyes to reality. God was just as able to clear my life of sin as He was to clear those heathen cities out of the Promised Land. He would enable me to put my foot on the neck of every weakness of character. That was the purpose of Christ living a flawless life, so He could pass it on to us. I simply had to allow Him to do it. Gradually I realized that I sometimes played games with myself and with God. I begged for deliverance, while a part of me was still hugging the sin. I began to pray, "Help me to let go of and truly hate my sins." Within the past few weeks He's given me a glorious victory, one long coveted. There are many more to go, but His

71

power and willingness are infinite. He will enable you to place your foot upon the necks of your hated sins too. Do not give up.

Joshua said to them, "Do not be afraid; do not be discouraged. Be strong and courageous. This is what the Lord will do to all the enemies you are going to fight" (Joshua 10:25).

Somebody's Son

It's amazing how one can remain detached from war until one has a son. It's possible to watch the worst atrocities with only an intellectual awareness of their horror. We are against war, of course—all that mindless killing and waste of life, to say nothing of money—yet newscasters monotone their tales of fighting in some far-off land almost nightly, and we give it less attention than the local weather forecast. We see the victims sprawled along the streets and hillsides of unfamiliar backdrops, but it's nothing to us as long as it keeps its distance.

We *don't* like seeing the troops in U.S. khaki. That's a bit too close to home. There was a dreadful television series called *Tour of Duty*, which depicted the Vietnam War more accurately than we care to acknowledge. I say it was terrible, for men (Caucasian and Asian alike) fell into the tropical shrubbery, bleeding and dying by the dozens. Those who were fortunate jostled off on stretchers to some bullet-ridden aid station, their bandages red with television's exhaustless supply of "blood." When I was unfortunate enough to be exposed to that particular drama, I had to keep reminding myself that it was *just television*, as every now and then the camera zoomed in on some tortured young face (an actor, you understand), and it became the face of *my* sons. Then for moments over which I had no control, they were *all* my son. They were *all* tall and thin with wheat-colored hair and brown eyes, haggard, afraid, and pursued by death. The bent, perspiring ones carrying the stretcher, the ones left dying in the sprawl of fatigues, the ones creeping cautiously through the unfamiliar hostile terrain.

Every one of them *was* somebody's son. Not those pseudo-soldiers enacting the nightmare to trigger America's adrenaline, but the real soldiers who did the real killing and the real dying in a real war. I selfishly bow my head and thank God I never had a son the right age at the right time.

There is a story of a Father who sent His Son upon a unique mission. There was no draft. The Youth volunteered. He went to save an entire nation, but the citizens were indifferent to their danger and counted Him an interloper. They treated Him shabbily at best, cruelly at worst. The Father had connections in high places and could have recalled His Son at any moment, but the cause was all-important to both of Them, and He asked for no concession, this young Warrior who went without weapon into battle.

Eventually they killed Him, the very ones He'd gone to rescue—not a quick, clean slaughter, but a slow, humiliating torture with dark, underlying factors depicting the total monstrous meaning of final death.

For a moment, consider the Father who watched Him taken captive, kicked, lashed, ridiculed, and finally murdered in the most obscene way. At one point the Youth cried out desperately, "Father, where *are* You?" and the Father, with full power to rescue, steeled Himself to silence. As a parent, try *that* scenario on for size.

Somewhere in the long quiet, the Son whispered through His agony, "It's OK, Dad," and He died. It's the parent part of me that dimly comprehends the cost of my salvation. I owe Them both everything, the Father and the Son. The story has a happy ending, for no grave could withstand such a team, and They are together now, waiting for you and me to join Them. This was not a tour of duty, but a tour of love. A gift of such magnitude that our human minds can but nibble at the edges of comprehension.

Stretch our hearts, Lord, to receive such love.

For God so loved the world that he gave his one and only Son, that whoever believes in him shall not perish but have eternal life (John 3:16).

73

Thank You, Lord, for Time Out

For three weeks I'd done nothing but work—good, hard, physical work. There had been raspberries to prune and all the prickly remains to cart away. Long overdue for care, my prayer garden had become an embarrassing jungle of last year's dead and shriveled blooms. Deadlines or no deadlines, my typewriter must idle while I tackled the more practical matters of life.

Then I thought about my plans for a new office. For years I'd camped temporarily in the corners of our children's bedrooms, in the attic, in the garage. Oh, that awful summer in the garage when squashed mosquitoes become the hallmark of my manuscripts!

Faced with our youngest son's impending return from college, I pondered where to go, for I'd been working in a corner of his cozy room. Oh, he'd have let me stay, but we cramped each other's style. I never felt terribly creative among his stereo, tape deck, speakers, and fat manuals on the technicalities of flying, and I'm sure my files and typewriter didn't inspire him.

All of a sudden one night, in the wee hours when sleep eluded me, I knew (and marveled that I had not known before) where I could go. In our great, hip-roofed red barn there was a small dark room that had once been a granary. Not a ray of light penetrated its four walls. Our children, with the help of a long extension cord, had used it for secret things—a clubhouse, a playhouse, a spooky place to sleep out with friends. Not liking its dark interior, I had counted it of little value, but now, in my moment of inspiration, the obvious occurred to me. A large window, of course!

Next day I called the carpenter, and busy though he was, he came on a rainy afternoon and cut the magic hole through which light poured into the darkness of a hundred years. After he had gone, I rolled back the heavy sliding door and could not believe my good fortune. The window overlooked our orchard and pond. Outside, a soft rain fell on green fields. My typewriter and I had found a home at last. A huge discarded workbench became the generous desk for which I'd always longed. Over it I hung my favorite pencil sketch of a Canada goose and her babies. Everything looked great against the wood walls, which had aged a lovely color. Here I would display shells, cones, dried flowers, baskets—all the natural things I had collected over the years.

It occurred to me, as I was hanging the "praying hands" plaque Mitch had made for me years before at camp that it was ironic, this room for me to work in—for I was tired of work. Tired of preparing talks when I wasn't a speaker by profession.

Let others who'd gulped down volumes on communication speak. You give a lot of yourself speaking—I don't know how preachers do it 52 times a year.

I was tired of being asked how many degrees I had and how I'd earned them. I didn't have any! I'd loved life, read everything I could get my hands on, suffered, raised children, sometimes trembled in wonder before the Almighty One, and sometimes trudged through far too many ordinary days. Mostly the Lord had educated me. But He never gave me a velvet hood to hang over my T-shirt and jeans.

And the writing. I'd worked all winter on a book manuscript that was now being evaluated. The criticism wasn't all positive. The parts I feared were not so good, they'd OK'd. The parts I liked best of all, they'd politely said must go. Ouch!

So why was I preparing this little nest in which to create? Creating involved hard work. Perhaps I should leave it to the young and the talented.

My joints ached. Pruning and spading flower beds after a winter of sedentary work had sent me limping toward a hot bath. For three weeks I'd not written a word. I'd even turned down an exciting invitation to speak in a far place. Maybe I'd not do those things anymore. Maybe I'd write only long, chatty letters to my friends (most of whom hadn't heard from me in months) in this special room, which was more mine than any room on earth had ever been.

I scoured the filthy wood of the floor until it returned at last to its natural color and grain. Along about the third coat of paste wax, down upon my knees, aching in every joint, I began to think about the book, the one the evaluators had roughed around. They'd complained about the opening. Suddenly I knew how to fix the opening, exactly how. I couldn't wait for the wax to dry. And that place where the conversation bogged down . . . maybe . . .

Thank You, God, for raspberry bushes and flower beds. And for floors to be scrubbed when the mind is weary. Thank You for putting the right balance into my life. And thanks for the new room, after all those moves, upstairs and down. I look forward to whatever You plan for me to do in it over the years.

Come to me, all you who are weary and burdened, and I will give you rest (Matt. 11:28).

Cross-country Flight

Our son, who pilots his own small plane, once told me that he didn't care much for winter flying, at least in our frigid corner of the country (western New York). The landscape was so bleak beneath him that he found it depressing.

I pondered what he said, for his mind and mine often touch and go on the same runways. Though I've done a fair amount of winter flying, all of it has been in large commercial jets soaring well above the weather. Reentry into the sleety reality of earth life has sometimes been scary, but always brief, with little time to analyze the countryside.

However, a few months ago I flew from San Francisco, California, to Rochester, New York, on a dismal midwinter day. For some reason, which the pilot did not deem necessary to disclose, we flew beneath the dark, threatening clouds rather than above them. Maybe there was no above that day. Maybe the shifting, wispy grayness thickened into infinity. At any rate, we rumbled relentlessly across America, hour after hour, with a bird's-eye view of the panorama below.

Foolishly I'd requested a window seat, forgetting how pinched and claustrophobic that position becomes on a cross-country flight. So whether I liked it or not, I had a window, and sheer boredom drove me to peer out occasionally. What I saw below brought back my son's comment in bold type. The Rockies, even on a sunny day, always give rise to uneasy speculation on my part. Every crash story I've ever read flashes across my mind as I look into their forsaken depths. I always wonder if I'd turn into a whimpering liability in a disaster, or if some heretofore undetected valor would surface to carry me through, even to make me useful. Today I did not wish to contemplate the grim details of an impromptu landing. I set myself to reading *Better Homes and Gardens* as though muffins and bathroom decor were essential to the long-range scheme of things upon our planet.

Later, when the mountains mellowed into plains that looked flat enough to accommodate a 747 almost anywhere, I allowed myself to observe the flow of earth beneath. Bleak, my son had said, but that word was inadequate to capture what I observed, though I couldn't think of a better one. The white land, broken roughly into huge rectangles, stretched desolate and terrible to the horizon. Here and there snow-covered humps hinted of houses and barns. No sign of life. No sun. Nothing moving.

To the college student who squirmed wearily beside me I said facetiously, "Do you suppose anyone's alive down there?"

"Don't look out," he advised. "It's too depressing."

He was right. For the first time I saw our planet as almost uninhabitable. I saw us as pitiful creatures in an environment that, if I hadn't fully believed the gospel, I'd have labeled abandoned.

I looked about at the smartly dressed, sophisticated occupants of the planet, reading, dozing, juggling weary babies, just getting where they were going, this trip only a hyphen in their frenetic lives. We were pathetic, all of us—as hopeless as if we wandered, lost and alone, in the desolation below. It is our permanent state, even when the sun shines and our hearts are bold and careless, for the sin condition lurks, persistent and forbidding, even on the brightest days.

Praise God, His Son breaks through the gloom of our lostness, shining with a light that cannot be dimmed. He will lead those who have sought Him to a city that has "no need of the sun, neither of the moon, to shine in it: for the glory of God [does] lighten it, and the Lamb is the light thereof" (Rev. 21:23, KJV).

I wished that day I could fling those words like a banner over the frozen earth, that humanity might look up in humble wonder at their deliverance from a dying planet by One whose cross was planted firmly in its lonely soil.

I am the light of the world (John 8:12).

Sacred Security System

This afternoon as I was folding laundry I listened to a Christian radio station broadcasting from Buffalo, New York. I hear many inspiring sermons and interesting discussions on this station. Sometimes I am uplifted by beautiful Christian music, and other times I turn it off because the sound is so raucous that I'm not sure whether I'm listening to a Christian broadcast or a rock concert.

But anyhow, this afternoon there was a call-in show, and the subject under discussion was mom's prayer groups for children in public schools.

It was exciting to hear the serious, dedicated voices of young mothers who called in to report that they were organizing, or attending, such a group already. They had a strong sense of the dangers surrounding their children as they returned once more to the halls of learning. Some noted that after driving their children to school, they simply met in a car at curbside and prayed for their little ones before returning home. It bodes well for America when parents exhibit such concern for the spiritual welfare of their children.

What of your children or your grandchildren? Is anyone praying for their protection? Perhaps you've raised them carefully. Their ears have never heard foul or profane language. Nor erotic innuendos. They've never seen a pornographic magazine nor even heard of one. It's quite possible they've never met hard, manipulative children who pretend to be friendly while using their innocent victim. You may have warned about drugs and alcohol, but until they face it themselves, your children little understand the power of peer pressure. (Fortunate your children if they attend a Christian school, but even there they will be tried and tempted.)

The world into which we send our children in this age is not a safe—or always pleasant—one. However well equipped the school and dedicated the teaching staff, there is often an undercurrent of evil thriving in the halls. Our children walk every day into this unsavory environment. How wise those mothers who do not underestimate the problem, who sense the need for intense prayer.

Consider the biblical picture of Job (Job 1:5). After his sons and daughters enjoyed periodic feastings, Job interceded for them. "Early in the morning he would sacrifice a burnt offering for each of them, thinking 'Perhaps my children have sinned and cursed God in their hearts.'" This was Job's regular custom.

I expect these children were young adults, yet Job still experienced a deep sense of responsibility for their salvation.

How comforting it is to know that we can actually put an invisible wall of protection about our sons and daughters, of whatever age, through prayer. It doesn't have to be group prayer, but surely God must bend low when He sees a small band of kneeling mothers and grandmothers storming heaven in behalf of their offspring.

Take a good look at your children today. That golden-haired little boy who hugs you hard before he races for the bus. The African-American child with his great, soft, dark eyes and sparkling grin. The dainty, sloe-eyed Oriental lass (I had one of those). Do you cherish them enough to enfold them in prayer? My own daily plea for our three sons and three daughters—all now adults—is that, in the name of Jesus, every evil power will be driven back and that the holy angels will form a ring of protection about them and that the Holy Spirit will come to each one like a cleansing flame. All through the day as I go about my work I lift up their individual needs to a God who loves to cooperate with praying mothers.

This is the best gift we can give our children. Those beautiful sons and daughters who fill our hearts with joy. And, oh yes, the grandchildren too, those precious little people!

In the morning, O Lord, you hear my voice; in the morning I lay my requests before you and wait in expectation (Ps. 5:3).

My Letter to Jesus

On this planet, Jesus, it's our custom to write thank-you notes. It's one of the nicer things we do, amid all the hate, prejudice, and fighting. This morning I realized I'd never written one to You, the Source of all my hope and happiness. (That's ironic, isn't it, but typical of our insensitivity here.) So here I am at my desk, frustrated that my earthbound brain can never do justice to what is in my heart.

If I could present this note in person, I'd bring it with a bouquet of white chrysanthemums, the shaggy ones that tumble all over my middle garden in September. If I had Your way with miracles, I'd bring You snowflakes and the smell of winter on a November day, for perhaps You don't have these exact wonders in heaven.

Just taking up the pen to start gives me an excited, happy feeling. I'll admit I'd like to think of You opening it literally and sitting down under a tree to read as I do when I wander back from the mailbox on sunny days, but You will get the message. I know that. In fact, perhaps You're smiling and reading over my shoulder right now.

A few days ago I stood at the window, getting ready to have my morning conversation with You. I'm not very conventional about this business of praying. You know there are times when I come to You face down on the floor—I am that desperate. At those times even my knees aren't a low enough approach. But this wasn't one of those days. As I watched the sun creep over the stubbled fields with their patches of snow, a gaudy male pheasant came strutting cautiously out of our spruce grove, crossed the road, and disappeared into a stand of red pines. A few moments later another followed. For 15 minutes pheasants, male and female, paraded at spaced intervals before my fascinated eyes. Oh, I've seen plenty of pheasants here at our farm. But somehow it was everything together, like a great work of art, only the sun patterns shifted, and there were movement and changing color. You don't get that in art. I didn't even say the usual things to You. I just stood there with a lump in my throat while You bade me, in Your own delightful, creative way, "Good morning, June. Have a nice day."

Then it hit me—the blackest, emptiest, loneliest thought I've ever had. What if shadows still patterned the fields, sun glistened on pines, pheasants swaggered across lawns—and there was no Jesus Christ? That would be unbearable pain.

In that awful moment on the cross when You cried out to Your Father, thinking He had forsaken You, You faced triumphantly—for all of us—the blackness, the finality of sin. Your eyes fell on people You loved, the tear-stained face of Your mother, the figure of John, who had become, for some reason, especially dear to You. Perhaps, even in Your agony, You looked out over the landscape and wondered if You'd ever again see sun and trees and shadows moving across the Temple walls. Most of all, Your heart must have broken for that Father whom You could not reach and that land which Your earthling brothers had never seen.

At the name of Jesus every knee should bow, in heaven and on earth and under the earth, and every tongue confess that Jesus Christ is Lord, to the glory of God the Father (Phil. 2:10, 11).

A New Look at Grief

We usually associate the word "grief" with death, or at least we think of death as the ultimate grief, heading a list of lesser sorrows.

Now I'm not so sure. Having tangled with close, hurting death in years past, I know about *that* kind of grief. Sometimes, years later, one hardly dares look on the scars for fear they are not healed.

But now I have faced a new brand of sorrow. A daily thing. When we lose someone we love it is an agonizing experience, but there is a finality about it. Life does go on, and we usually stagger along with it, moving through the phases of adjustment.

But a daily grief—one to which one wakes every morning—what does one do with that? My first reaction was to hide. Like an injured animal, I wanted only a dark burrow within which to lick my wounds.

I would, I decided, turn to the outdoors. Never had I failed to find healing there. I would walk and walk until the redness of sumac and the softness of sun made me whole again. But I only hurt the more. September was a mockery, for this grief I had in some measure brought upon myself. Not deliberately. Not through intentional sin. But through unwise decisions, wrong turns in an unfamiliar road. So all that the outdoors said to me was "Get back in your burrow. You don't deserve sunlight dancing over fields of winter wheat. You are guilty, guilty, guilty!"

In desperation I began to look around. Was anyone weeping, except at funerals? Or even more specifically, were any weeping who had brought grief, knowingly or otherwise, upon themselves? I was looking for men and women who hurt as I did, and who would have to go right on hurting without any immediate solution. And I found them.

There was Bill, the idealist, who watched a dream shatter at his feet. He wept, and men don't cry, you know. He blamed himself. His agony was real. It matched mine, perhaps surpassed it. I watched, for Bill and God are friends. Would Bill tunnel into his own private burrow, no longer sure where he stood in earth or heaven? No. Very carefully, through his tears, he picked up the pieces of the fragile, lovely thing he'd valued and lost. He began to build again. (Knowing Bill, I'd guess he did most of the building on his knees.) You won't believe this, but what he's creating from the fragments has a vulnerable beauty surpassing the original. (If you're annoyed because I'm not being very specific in these stories, let me assure you it's because they aren't lived-happily-ever-after stories from the past, but moment-by-moment battles from the now. Thus I'm limited in how much I can share.)

Then there is Kate, who has tried in every way she knows how to put a shaky marriage back together. Finally, in despair, she dumped the whole mess in God's lap, feeling sure He had a happy ending filed away somewhere in the heavenly office. Months passed. Nothing happened. No miracle. At last it dawned on Kate that she simply had to walk in faith, doing the best she could with each new morning, accepting what she could not change. Again I watched. Having knocked on the door of heaven and received no audible reply, would she assume no one was there? When a few days ago she told me, "I'm eager to learn whatever God has to teach me from all this," I had my answer.

I believe that God accepts us, mistakes and all. That He can even use our errors as growing tools for us, and that He does indeed have happy endings in the heavenly office for those of us who have fully committed ourselves to Him. But we sometimes have to wait for them. To relax and trust Him. And to lay aside our grief. For grief denies the power of God to bring good out of evil.

I wonder. Can I personally appropriate this greatest of all lessons? Can I struggle up out of the darkness, along with Bill and Kate, daring to believe God is equal to any tangled mess we bring Him? I do not know. I have never before been put to such a test. But yesterday, when I saw a cardinal flashing from limb to limb in a Norway spruce, my heart leaped with an old familiar joy. That's a good sign, isn't it?

Do not be afraid of what you are about to suffer. . . . Be faithful, even to the point of death, and I will give you the crown of life (Rev. 2:10).

A Tale of Two Gardens

Four years ago I decided to fulfill an old dream by creating a large perennial garden in an area adjacent to our country road. Already there was a stand of red pines just waiting to become a backdrop.

When my husband tilled the area, however, I realized I had assumed a project of major proportions. Because the garden would be part of a spacious lawn area, it had to be on a grand scale. It was now up to me to rake out all grass and weeds.

Under the scorching August sun I began, eagerly at first, wearily all too soon. When I felt I couldn't stand another minute of it, I looked around to see what I'd accomplished. As I viewed the tiny square I'd cleared, in comparison with the vast expanse remaining, I didn't know whether to laugh or cry.

My first thought was born of desperation. *Well, I'll just throw grass seed over it all, and the fall rains will soon return the whole mess to lawn. I must have been insane to think I could landscape such an area!*

But somehow, that solution was not my style. I was well aware that anything of real value always costs us something. It also dawned on me, there in the dirt and sweat, that there is a moment in every worthwhile achievement in which one is tempted to cast it all aside. Only those who move beyond that point experience the joy of real accomplishment.

So I sat down under the pines, had a cup of water, daydreamed a bit about the end results, and took up my rake once more.

Today I toured the entire expanse, enjoyed the airy Russian sage, fuzzy lamb's ears, and artemisia. Lavender petunias moved like a stream through the silvers and grays, all the soft colors lovely against old rocks we had diligently dragged from hedgerows. I can see now that I would have missed much had I decided to give up on that hot August day.

Jesus, also, having set Himself to the greatest challenge ever witnessed by the universe, faced a moment of decision, a moment when He longed to quit. The nightmare ahead seemed more than the frail humanity, which encumbered His divinity, could endure. We can never grasp the hell He glimpsed as He leaned over the abyss of His commitment. His coming separation from His Father *felt* permanent.

"Father," He cried out, "everything is possible for you. Take this cup from me" (Mark 14:36).

That was the moment of despair, but praise God, He did not abandon His dream. When He added the final phrase, "yet not what I will, but what you will" (verse 36), He set His eye upon the goal and never looked back. What He endured in the following 24 hours is beyond our comprehension, but He did not falter.

No matter how dark your day, or mine, we have hope because of *His* day of decision. I expect to spend all eternity in a state of gratitude for that one moment when the God-Man wrestled with *His* personal challenge in a shadowed garden long ago.

They went to a place called Gethsemane. . . . And he began to be deeply distressed and troubled (Mark 14:32, 33).

Breakthrough!

There's something good happening in our country. Something to tuck in amid the awful headlines. The other day as I was sitting in a large airport—awaiting departure and observing humanity—I saw a father and son saying goodbye. Son staying, dad leaving. Dad looked like a man of the Kansas wheat fields. Medium height, but strong. Like he'd seen a lot of sun and a lot of ups and downs. The youth had inherited his tight, wiry build, but he was a bit taller and didn't have the look of the land about him.

As the loudspeaker herded passengers aboard, dad stuck his hand out awkwardly to son. Son ignored the hand, enfolding his father in a great lingering bear hug. Dad walked away looking a little shaken, a little shy, but I'll bet his weary shoulders feel the imprint of those loving arms yet.

In the father I saw the composite of all my generation. We hugged and cuddled our little ones with tender affection, but there always came a day when it was no longer macho for dads and sons to hug, and even mom felt a little shy of these young folks she'd nurtured into adulthood. Maybe they didn't want to be hugged anymore. Instead of being the center of their worlds, the one upon whom they doted, she was just an ordinary woman with flaws and faults, whom they no longer saw through such starry eyes. It took courage to hug a grown child.

On the same trip, however, I observed another heartwarming little vignette. Mother and daughter this time. Mother staying, daughter leaving. Mother elderly, misshapen, gray fuzzy perm, blue raincoat, matronly shoes. Tired face. Daughter chic, just downright chic. Bangle earrings, and that sleek look some young women manage, I know not how. It was hard to believe she had sprung from the parent beside her.

Again the loudspeaker sorted families, and mother and daughter prepared to part. Mom stood, looking almost dazed, whether with grief or wonder that she had produced this radiant being before her. She made no move toward her offspring, but the young woman took her mother's wrinkled face in both hands and looked deep into her eyes. "I love you," she said. "Don't you ever forget that. A little bit of you goes with me, you know, always and forever."

Wow!

When the prodigal returned home, you recall, the father "threw his arms around him and kissed him" (Luke 15:20). Evidently in those long-ago times a display of affection was considered normal behavior. Where did we lose it?

But those two demonstrations of filial love, both in one day, made me proud of our 1990s young people. They are more open, more demonstrative, freer to express what's in their hearts.

My headline for the day would read:
BREAKTHROUGH! NEW GENERATION KNOWS HOW TO SHOW AFFECTION. MAYBE OLD GENERATION CAN LEARN. HOPE FOR THE WORLD.

Now Israel's eyes were failing because of old age, and he could hardly see. So Joseph brought his sons close to him, and his father kissed them and embraced them (Gen. 48:10).

Leave Us Gently, Summer

The butterfly days of summer are flitting, one by one, toward autumn. Along about mid-July I begin to clutch at them. There are all too few summers in any lifetime.

When the children were small I'd look at them on waning August days and suddenly realize they'd soon be off to school, leaving another September nibbling away at my motherhood. I would put aside everything else, concentrating on the sheer joy of their presence.

At that time my husband played golf on Tuesdays after work, leaving us alone for the supper hour. We made it picnic night, the children and I, and we'd pack a lunch and set off on foot for some favorite spot right on our own property. Once we baked potatoes, boiled corn, and even made a pie. After wrapping everything in foil, we trudged off to the woods, where we sat on an old log and ate our crazy "hot picnic." We were lazy and carefree. I haven't felt that way in a long time.

I wasn't always a relaxed mother (I can hear my children's hearty amens!), but somehow at the end of summer on those lush and sultry days, I'd glimpse the glory and transiency of parenthood.

It seems too often now that summers for me are only a blur of wet towels from the pond, cleaning up the kitchen after endless meals (everyone's on a different schedule), putting the house to rights between the arrivals and departures of assorted guests, and squeezing mini-vacations into the erratic household agenda.

We haven't had a real vacation in several years, what with summer jobs, summer school courses, and the eternal debate over where to go . . . Amy likes a mountain lake, Lori likes the sea, Mitchell likes big cities, and no one queries me.

Nevertheless, when the wheat begins to ripen and the last of the summer fashions flutter in the hot breezes of sidewalk sales, I am seized with the sweetness of the season. I want no more kitchen duty and no more guests who somehow managed vacations despite obstacles.

That doesn't mean I get my wish. The household doesn't come to a screeching halt just because I suddenly hunger to live by moments instead of days. Life continues on its hurly-burly way, dragging me with it, as I snatch small souvenirs of summer—a glittering spider's web in the early morn, a letter at noon to read in the shade of old maples, and a few stolen moments at dusk in the prayer garden behind our barn where white impatiens glow like small stars in the gathering dark.

I ponder: If given one day to myself at summer's end, just how would I spend it? First, at sunrise I'd bicycle around a familiar five-mile block, stopping at the old cemetery to watch morning sift over the rolling pasture where sheep graze. I'd come home to breakfast on cold melon and Amy's homemade whole-wheat English muffins.

Then I'd go to the pond and lie on the dock, taking no pen, no pad, no book. I would do nothing except listen to the small waterfall that feeds into the pond, and let the sun melt summer's havoc within me. (Oh, come on now, June, you know that no matter how inert your body, your mind races on, planning the Sabbath guest menu, outlining an overdue article, deciding if the children have adequate wardrobes for school. There's no place to hide from the complexities of a busy life.)

OK, but before I give up my special day, I shall take my Bible and sit down to read for 30 minutes. It's more effective than sunlight, cheaper than travel, and it feeds all my deepest needs. Honest, that peace bit is for real (John 14:27; Ps. 26:3).

Another load of towels in the dryer, lasagna in the freezer for Sabbath, and just enough time to clip the grass along the front walk. Walk me through the day, Jesus. The season doesn't really matter.

He will quiet you with his love (Zeph. 3:17).

Faith, Marital and Divine

Once, when doing a detailed study of Christ's earthly years, I became intensely aware of His obsession with faith. He seemed ever appalled at the lack of it and delighted when He occasionally stumbled upon it. It was startling to discover that He could help only those who believed.

Since then I have accumulated many texts and quotations relating to the subject, but it was a few statements from a book by Morris Venden that further stimulated my thinking on the matter.

"Faith is trusting another. The moment you have faith, you have at least two parties. You cannot have faith with only one. Furthermore, faith is one individual depending upon another. How does that happen? First of all, you must have someone trustworthy; and second, you must get to know him. Only then will you trust spontaneously and naturally" (*Obedience of Faith*, pp. 20, 21).

I asked myself what human being I trusted most. It didn't take much deliberation for me to decide that it was my husband. There are others in whom I place considerable confidence, but faith in my husband is the result of two years of courtship and 45 years of marriage. That is pretty solid ground.

Sometimes when he travels to a distant city on business I go along. He drops me off in the downtown area to shop and then drives away to meet his appointments for the day.

I am always a little uneasy when he disappears into the maze of heavy traffic. I feel alone on the unfamiliar street corner. But I know he will return at 5:00 in the afternoon to pick me up. I can shop all day without a moment of concern, for the familiar car will drive up to the curb at the appointed time, and the familiar face will smile its pleasure in our being together again.

If he's a bit late, I know it is because his appointments ran longer than he expected. I need only be patient. He will arrive. He will forget neither me nor our place of meeting. Never has he failed a rendezvous in 45 years. So I have total faith, built on long, positive experience, in his performance.

A few years ago I underwent major surgery. Coming out of anesthesia is not one of life's better moments. It gives a whole new dimension to the word "sick." For a few days I did not want to see anybody. Not my friends, not my fellow church members, not even my children. Only Don.

I was too ill to talk to him, but I wanted him to sit by my bed and read and offer comfort when I moaned and complained. Through my haze of misery, I wanted to see his familiar outline engrossed in the *Wall Street Journal*. As long as he was there, I had faith that the nightmare would end eventually, and we would take up our normal lives again.

How had I come to this place where one person, out of earth's billions, merited my total trust, my total love? Where I wanted him with me in the worst and best of times? Where I was confident he would act for my good whatever the cost?

Author Venden had said, "Faith is trusting another." He was right. And the only way we can develop the kind of trust in Jesus that so delighted Him 2,000 years ago (and still does) is to have the same close, caring, sharing, everyday relationship with Him that I have with my husband, and that has evolved through finding him totally trustworthy.

Could I put that kind of trust in Someone I had never seen? Could I wait for Him on the street corner of time and know He would come without fail? In the darkest moments of my life, could I be at peace because He was there beside me?

Only if He was my constant companion, as my husband has been. Only if I'd tried Him again and again and found Him true. Only if His Word had become part of my thought pattern, and my prayertime as natural as breathing. It would be harder, much harder, than knowing my husband, who comes home each evening and who is ever so tangible. But everything, according to Jeremiah 29:13, hinges on it. Everything.

Though you have not seen him, you love him; and even though you do not see him now, you believe in him and are filled with an inexpressible and glorious joy (1 Peter 1:8).

How Plants (and People) Grow

Everyone marvels at my indoor ferns. I have to admit they are luxuriant and a healthy deep green. Dozens of tiny new fronds curl up from their centers, reminding me that the huge pots they are in won't do forever.

My friends say, "Where did you get those ferns? They must have cost you a fortune."

"No," I reply modestly, "they all came from the grocery store or the farmer's market. I spent no more than $4 or $5 apiece. They were small, and some of them were a bit sickly when I bought them."

"Well, what do you do to them? Out with it. What's your secret?"

"I water them once a week and fertilize them each month. That's all."

They don't believe me because that's what they do to their ferns, but with less startling results. They walk away muttering, sure I'm withholding some botanical magic. And I am. But it isn't anything I do to them. The ferns are grouped in one corner of our family room. One hangs in a large macramé planter, another sits on the floor, and yet another falls like a green fountain from a wicker plant stand.

It so happens that two walls of floor-to-ceiling windows, facing east and south, meet in that corner, which means the plants gain full benefit of light and sun from daybreak to dusk. They in fact receive a lot more sun then I ever dreamed ferns could tolerate. In this bright atmosphere they thrive.

There you are, my friends. I can take no credit, you see, for this green miracle. The blessing comes to the ferns all apart from their own efforts or mine. They escape mediocrity only through their prolonged exposure to a mysterious, intangible source of nourishment that they can never comprehend.

Sometimes my friends ask me another kind of question, totally unrelated to houseplants. "June," they say, discouragement tingeing their words, "I've been a Christian all these years and nothing's happening. I have the same old sins, and I feel so lethargic spiritually. What am I doing wrong?"

I can relate to that. I've been in that situation myself more times than I like to recall. But there is an answer, and now that I think about it, it isn't so unrelated to ferns after all.

To produce specimen ferns—or specimen Christians—certain simple procedures must take place on a regular basis. You can't water and fertilize a fern spasmodically.

The same applies to the spiritual nature, only more so. A fern can go a week without attention. Not so the soul. It requires daily nourishment from the Word of God. Otherwise, the sinful nature asserts its right to rule, and we find ourselves reverting to a pale, sickly experience. Daily Bible study is such a simple, undramatic solution, but then, so is watering a plant.

Now comes the exciting part. The break from mediocrity. But you can't get to that point without the faithful, daily scriptural nurturing, so never skip that stage. (It wouldn't do my ferns a bit of good to hang in the window corner if I didn't feed and water them. A dead fern isn't much benefited by sunlight.)

If the miracle of Light (please note the capital L) is going to happen in your spiritual life and mine, we must be sure we're hanging in the "window corners" of religious experience. I would say, spiritually speaking, that would include a quiet place of unhurried prayer every day, the gatherings of God's people midweek and on the Sabbath, and periods of ministry with the sick and discouraged. The more exposure to the Light, the more growth.

Then something mysterious and wonderful can begin to take place. Label it "victorious living." Fronds of fruitful service spring out of our new life. Because we have nourished our feeble spiritual natures with the Bread of Life and hung ourselves in the "window corner" of prayer, the glorious light of the Holy Spirit is freed to release power upon our indifferent, sin-loving hearts, and as unconsciously as any fern, we'll develop a luxuriant Christlikeness.

In my book that beats raising houseplants any day.

He is like the light of morning at sunrise (2 Sam. 23:4).

Prescription for Depression

Jeremiah, like David, was melancholic. He experienced agonizing despair.

> "Cursed be the day I was born!
> May the day my mother bore
> not be blessed!" (Jer. 20:14).

> "Why did I ever come out of the womb
> to see trouble and sorrow
> and to end my days in shame?" (verse 18).

There were times when he felt totally abandoned by God.

> "Even when I call out or
> cry for help, he shuts out my
> prayer" (Lam. 3:8).

> "Like a bear lying in wait,
> like a lion in hiding,
> he dragged me from the path
> and mangled me
> and left me without help" (verses 10, 11).

His expectations were dashed.

> "I have been deprived of peace;
> I have forgotten what prosperity is.
> So I say, 'My splendor is gone
> and all that I had hoped from the
> Lord' " (verses 17, 18).

Yet in the very next breath Jeremiah spoke the steady words that end this reading.

Because I am melancholic, Lamentations 3 has taught me a great lesson. One of the flaws in the melancholic temperament is that we become depressed very easily (though the truth is Jeremiah had plenty to be depressed about) and can wallow in self-pity for days on end.

But there is another trait melancholics possess, which compensates. We are unswervingly loyal. Out of Jeremiah's pain and disillusionment, black as night, rose a candle, penetrating the gloom with its soft glow. That candle was Jeremiah's loyalty. However contradictory the circumstances, or even his own verbal outbursts, deep in his heart Jeremiah trusted God. He trusted Him because he knew His character.

Thus, in the midst of his own pity party, suddenly his loyalty thrust from him those honest words: "His compassions never fail. They are new every morning. . . . Men are not cast off by the Lord forever" (verses 22-31).

I too have felt abandoned by God at times in my life, but I could never walk away from Him, for like Jeremiah, I am committed for all time to serving Him. And even when all the evidence seems to the contrary, deep in my heart I too know He will bring good out of evil, victory out of failure, and order out of chaos.

When you find yourself slipping into depression, read Lamentations 3 and let Jeremiah's stubborn loyalty invade your despair. We need to learn to put our trust in the character and promises of God, rather than in the deceiving events of our day-to-day existence. Only thus will we journey safely into that land where no veil separates us from full truth and understanding.

> **Because of the Lord's great love we**
> **are not consumed,**
> **for his compassions never fail.**
> **They are new every morning. . . .**
> **I say to myself, "The Lord is my portion;**
> **therefore I will wait for him.". . .**
> **It is good to wait quietly for**
> **the salvation of the Lord. . . .**
> **For men are not cast off by the Lord forever.**
> **Though he brings grief he will show compassion,**
> **so great is his unfailing love.**
> **For he does not willingly bring**
> **affliction or grief to the children of men**
> > **(Lam. 3:22-33).**

A Place to Hide My Heart

At a writers' workshop I attended, the speaker asked how many kept journals. To her surprise, nearly every hand went up. I concluded that probably writers have more of a tendency to record their lives than the general public. If something's on our mind, putting it on paper helps sort it out. I don't deduce from this, however, that those whose skills lie in other fields should not keep a journal.

Right here, perhaps we should differentiate between a journal and a diary. There are those who keep a hasty record of the weather and the day's activities. A typical entry might read:

"Went to dentist. He says molar must come out. Ugh! Need rain. Picked first sweet corn. Jenny got a B on her history test."

That's better than nothing, but it's not a journal. In a journal one shares a great deal more of oneself. You can share as little or as much of your personal life as you wish. The book is for your eyes only. It's a place to record the burdens that you do not wish to inflict on others, the joys that fill your heart to bursting. It's OK to say, "I feel so hurt by Mother's phone call" or "I felt ridiculously pleased today when Joe noticed my new dress."

But it's even better to toss such thoughts around a bit. Regarding your mother's phone call, your journal might continue, "It seems like Mother and I have never been able to communicate well. I think we both long to be close, but when she comes at me in her accusing way, I simply withdraw into my shell and let her words bounce off me. I guess I've been doing it since I was a little girl. It was how I survived. Maybe now if I told her, gently, how much it hurts, she'd try to change. I'm not sure I could do that. I feel just like a little girl again when she starts berating me. Scared."

At that point you might decide to make the scarred relationship a matter of special prayer or even to seek counseling. Or, strangely enough, you might find that just writing it down clarified the problem sufficiently so you could talk with your mother about it.

But analyzing troublesome emotions is only one purpose, among many, of a journal. Probably its greatest benefit comes as you share your growing relationship with God or maybe even sometimes your frustrations with Him. (He can handle that.) There are those who have a spiritual journal in place of, or in addition to, a personal journal. I prefer to combine the two. I find that my spiritual life and my ordinary, everyday life are one.

I must admit that I don't write in it every day (though I would like to), but as often as possible—maybe every two or three weeks—I sit down and take time to analyze on paper where I've been and where I'm heading.

As I go back through my journals, I often note a thread of gloom weaving throughout the entries. I'm well aware that this springs from my melancholy temperament. (If you don't know about the four temperaments, rush out to the nearest Christian bookstore and buy Florence Littauer's *Personality Plus*.) I decided, as an antidote, to make a book of hope. In this book I collected encouraging Bible verses, upbeat quotations, and answers to prayer. I have illustrated this book with bits of art and lovely nature pictures to delight the eye. When I find myself smack in the middle of a pity party, I really do get the book out and let it remind me how foolish I am to dwell on negatives.

I also keep a garden journal. (I am first a child of God; second, a wife and mother; third, a writer; and fourth, a gardener. Sometimes the sequence of items 3 and 4 shifts.) It's a wonderful book, providing spaces for three years of notes alongside each other on the open page so that the gardener can compare what's going on in his or her little Eden year by year. I count it a great discovery. (Louis Carter and Joanne Lawson, *The Three-Year Garden Journal*. Starwood Publishers, P.O. Box 40503, Washington, D.C. 20016.)

Remember those pretty cloth-covered blank books you saw at the stationery store? Well, now you have an excuse to buy one.

Then the Lord said to Moses, "Write this on a scroll as something to be remembered" (Ex. 17:14).

Thad's Discovery

Friends had invited me to share their lunch. We sat around a small table beneath the trees at high noon on a hot August day. With us was our host's small grandson. We were all at camp meeting—a real old-fashioned camp meeting complete with sprawling main tent surrounded by neat rows of cabins, RVs, and small tents housing those in attendance.

Five-year-old Thad had spent golden days singing praises to his friend Jesus, listening to delightful stories, and playing in the sandbox with a brand-new set of friends. Now, here on the Sabbath, with some of his favorite adults, he poured Mott's applesauce onto his paper plate, rim to rim. While we gasped, he lifted the first spoonful of the cool delicacy to his lips, savored it lingeringly, and said dreamily to no one in particular, "I just love life."

We smothered our smiles.

"You're right, Thad," I said. "It's hard to beat applesauce and camp meeting and a cool breeze."

I knew exactly what he was talking about, this golden-haired child with the enormous blue eyes. Life didn't get much better than this. I too had lived in a kind of premature "heaven" all week. The small room to which I'd been assigned was simplicity itself. A bed, a desk, a chest of drawers, a large fan with which to combat the heat. That was all. I was glad to abandon, temporarily, the two-story colonial that is our home, with its complexity of rooms and all their accoutrements gathered over the years. I found the stark room with its pictureless white walls restful. No guilt over cluttered closets, unwashed windows, and hasty meals. The cafeteria served a wide selection of simple, healthful food that I ate in the company of old and dear friends.

There were no decisions, no temptations, no annoyances, and no deadlines.

I had come to this place to focus on God. To learn at the feet of those schooled in His Word. To pray with friends. I'd not been disappointed. We'd opened the Bible in intense study, sung "We Shall Behold Him" like a mighty chorus under the big tent, and gathered in small groups to pray.

Yes, I knew just what Thad was talking about. It was as close to heaven as he and I would ever get on this earth. In his childish innocence he sensed that. The awareness forced from him that strangely adult observation "I just love life." What he really loved was this moment of total rightness in a world that is too often topsy-turvy.

He wanted to stay, and so did I. Here with God and the applesauce and the singing. But it was nearly over. Two more meetings. One more song session in the summer dusk with God's gentle people, and then we'd all load our luggage into our waiting cars and head for the freeway and home.

For heaven is yet to come. In the meantime, there are ordinary and profound tasks awaiting us. There are floors to be scrubbed, children to be raised, cars to be built, and computers to be programmed. Music to be written and houses to be framed. Habits to be changed. Tempers to be tamed. Marriages to be celebrated, and deaths to be mourned. Most urgent of all, a slumbering world to be told of a soon-coming King.

And then there will be an eternity for the applesauce kid—and anyone else who's grown to cherish the friendship of the King—to explore the far reaches of His universe with no sense of time running out.

The urgency of this current year, however, is to dwell in His sweet presence until we are utterly homesick for His arrival. Let nothing distract us.

There is nothing better for men than to be happy and do good while they live. That everyone may eat and drink, and find satisfaction in all his toil—this is the gift of God (Eccl. 3:12, 13).

Seeking Solitude

I was the mother of several small children when I first read Anne Morrow Lindbergh's *Gift From the Sea*. I cherish it as one of the outstanding reading experiences of my book-strewn career.

At the time of writing, the author had been freed from all home responsibilities to spend two weeks at the beach alone. It had been so long since I'd been alone. My days, stacked end to end, were filled with the endless ups and downs of child-raising. Don worked hard to provide for us, and he cherished every moment of our time together.

But I longed for short snatches of privacy in which to restore myself. I'm the product of a solitary childhood. Perhaps that's the reason. I early wandered alone amid woods and field in a corner of the earth that had not yet been invaded by civilization. Or perhaps it's because I grew up among a reserved people. We didn't poke and pry about in each other's minds as is the current trend.

During those years of our marriage, when our children were small and dear and demanding, I'd sometimes lie in bed a bit before sleeping and imagine myself in a tiny cottage by the sea. I could even hear the waves breaking on the sand. I would pretend I had two days (*days*, please note, not weeks) in which to think, walk the shore, and perhaps put a few of my thoughts down on paper. It helped a little.

Eventually the children all went off to school. The house was very still between 8:00 a.m. and 4:00 p.m. I found I still knew how to do things besides cook oatmeal and cure colds. The quiet was healing, and I could offer my family a whole person when they came trooping in at night.

Years passed, and our family—nearly grown—was in a state of transition. Sons and daughters came and went from boarding schools, lived at home and worked, tried their wings and fluttered, temporarily, back to the nest. Not only was the house seldom empty, but it was helter-skelter with overlapping schedules. After the long, orderly, quiet years, I found myself retreating once more to that imaginary cabin by the sea.

From the vantage point of more than 60 years, I know there are many who require varying degrees of privacy to function efficiently. If the Christian woman (or man also, for that matter) wishes to grow in her (or his) relationship with Christ, there must be stillness for meditation, time to find God in the outdoors, opportunity to match one's pace with His majestic rhythms.

Eda LeShan, in an article for *Woman's Day* (May 1975), says: "I was shocked to discover that I'd married a man who needed to be alone—a man who did not want to tell me everything he was thinking, feeling, or doing. The more I clung and probed, the more he struggled to be free; the more he succeeded, the more threatened and outraged I became. . . .

"When I began to value myself more, my moments alone became precious. And the more I respected my own need for privacy, the less threatened I felt by my husband's need for autonomy. Now when we go our separate ways, we share ambivalent feelings; we both feel bereft and sad, but eager and alive to adventure. And when we get back together again, it is with joy and no sense of entrapment."

It's often hard to tell our families "I need some time alone," but as they see the value we place upon private moments with God, perhaps it will inspire them to seek that rich experience for themselves.

After he had dismissed them, he went up on a mountainside by himself to pray (Matt. 14:23).

God Can Use You—Guaranteed

Three of us were ministering at a women's retreat, one musically, one in conducting a seminar, and another as the speaker. Between our duties we met for conversational prayer. Though our main purpose was to seek the Holy Spirit's power for the small prayer groups that were convening in other areas, eventually, as we began to know and trust each other, we hesitantly lifted up some of our own needs.

After one session we looked at each other in wonder, realizing we were, all three of us, women who hated to leave home and family, who felt unsure of our abilities and who had suffered real trauma at various points in our lives. We laughed, a little shakily, at this God who took broken, ordinary women and used them. We felt very humble and very thankful He didn't send us out alone, but walked with us through the scary places, and gave us the sense to know we were utterly helpless without His Holy Spirit.

Why does God choose such common folk? Why did Jesus choose uneducated fishermen with whom to win the world? *The Desire of Ages* sheds some light on this subject: "They were humble and unlearned men, those fishers of Galilee; but Christ, the light of the world, was abundantly able to qualify them for the position for which He had chosen them. The Saviour did not despise education; for when controlled by the love of God, and devoted to His service, intellectual culture is a blessing. But He passed by the wise men of His time, because they were so self-confident that they could not sympathize with suffering humanity, and become colaborers with the Man of Nazareth. In their bigotry they scorned to be taught by Christ. The Lord Jesus seeks the cooperation of those who will become unobstructed channels for the communication of His grace. The first thing to be learned by all who would become workers together with God is the lesson of self-distrust; then they are prepared to have imparted to them the character of Christ. This is not to be gained through education in the most scientific schools. It is the fruit of wisdom that is obtained from the divine Teacher alone.

Jesus chose unlearned fishermen because they had not been schooled in the traditions and erroneous customs of their time. They were men of native ability, and they were humble and teachable—men whom he could educate for His work" (pp. 249, 250).

I've always felt sure God could use anyone dynamically in one area or another, if that individual would trust totally in Him and be much in prayer and study of the Word. It's important also to fulfill each small assignment as it comes along to the best of one's ability. If you're called to teach in a children's division, be innovative. Put your heart into it. Ask the Holy Spirit to impart spiritual vitality to your planning and to the hearts of your students. Follow this plan in every assignment, whether large or small. Remember, nothing ever happens without the quickening of the Holy Spirit. We may wax ever so eloquent, but without the Spirit, no lives will be transformed. Perhaps usefulness depends more than anything else on an understanding of our own helplessness.

"He who loves Christ the most will do the greatest amount of good. There is no limit to the usefulness of one who, by putting self aside, makes room for the working of the Holy Spirit upon his heart, and lives a life wholly consecrated to God. . . .

"God takes men as they are, and educates them for His service, if they will yield themselves to Him. The Spirit of God, received into the soul, will quicken all its faculties. Under the guidance of the Holy Spirit, the mind that is devoted unreservedly to God develops harmoniously, and is strengthened to comprehend and fulfill the requirements of God" (*Ibid.*, pp. 250, 251).

It's exciting to follow God's leading through the unknown and unexpected, letting Him reveal our potential in Him. If you've not tried it yet, start today.

Do not let this Book of the Law depart from your mouth; meditate on it day and night. . . . Then you will be prosperous and successful. . . . Be strong and courageous. . . . For the Lord your God will be with you wherever you go (Joshua 1:8, 9).

God Too Knows Pain

I awoke in the soft darkness of country night. No streetlights. No traffic. Only the occasional creaking of our old, old house and a faint whispering of wind about the window. Silence embroidered with peace—only the peace evaded me.

Our family had been struck down with tragedy. A staggering, frightening physical blow attacked one of our grown children with no warning, no apology. We wrestled with unaccustomed emotions. Fear, sadness, and, I suspect, a hint of anger. There was no reason. No explanation. No guarantees. It just happened. Too bad. That's life. Never mind that all the sun and laughter had gone out of our days. I did the daily tasks like a wind-up toy, numb and empty. I talked and smiled and cooked and shopped, but when left to myself I wept endlessly, unable to fit the inscrutable will of God into my aching heart.

Three weeks later our phone rang again, reporting that one soon to become a member of our family, and precious to our hearts, had been in a terrible auto accident. It could have snuffed out her young life, but left her instead battered, broken, and bleeding.

Never before had we driven toward a hospital with every breath a prayer. Never had we seen the blood of one close to us spattered over the inside of a car. Never had we looked down on a loved face, pale, stitched, and bruised.

Now here, in the middle of the night, I was alone with the God of my life. We'd always been good friends, God and I, even through the hard places. But this night I hurt so much that I could not relate properly to Him. What did He know of the pain in my heart, this God who walked the serene and unsullied streets of Paradise?

Out of habit, I attacked insomnia with Scripture.

"For God so loved the world . . ."

For the first time in my life I wondered. Maybe He loved us in a detached, remote way, but what did He care about my pillow wet with tears? The story of sin was too long and bitter. It involved too much pain. I could hardly bear my little corner of it, much less grasp some eternal love that encompassed the unnumbered horrors of life on a fallen planet.

". . . that he gave his only begotten Son . . ."

A very personal act, I had to admit. Nothing detached here. He, too, saw a Son suffer. Maybe sometimes He, too, thought the sin process too complex. Too long. Too agonizing. Maybe His paternal pillow was sometimes wet with tears. He had seen a beloved face "disfigured beyond that of any man and his form marred beyond human likeness" (Isa. 52:14). So whatever this long brutal process ravaging the centuries was all about, He was in it with us.

". . . that whosoever believeth in him . . ."

That was it. Through it all, thousands of years of humans weeping in the night, there was a golden thread that interlaced the grieving. Simple trust in Him who will come and wipe away all tears from our eyes. It's only when we lose the golden thread that the darkness closes in. In the meantime, "all things work together for good to them that love God" (Rom. 8:28, KJV). I struggled to get hold of that, hurting humanity resisting divine wisdom. "Help me rest in that promise," I prayed. "It's so hard. I'm not sure I'm able to internalize it. It skims the surface of my consciousness like a mindless nursery rhyme. This pain, this shock, this ongoing fear—it will work for good? Could it be? Is that the golden thread passed on to me by a million Christian sufferers? Show me how to place it gently in the hands of my hurting children."

". . . should not perish, but have everlasting life" (John 3:16, KJV).

Show me, Lord, the divine perspective, the long grand sweep of eternity. But never let me forget, either, the vignette of paternal pain upon Golgotha.

I will not forget you! See, I have engraved you on the palms of my hands (Isa. 49:15, 16).

A Lesson From Lisa

We were in the midst of a family dinner, 13 of us gathered about our long, long table in the dining area. Sons, daughters, in-laws, and grandchildren. Our two small granddaughters sat in their customary places, one on my right, the other on my left. Jenny, just turned 8, very grown-up and eager to help clear away the dinner plates and serve the raspberry pie. Lisa, 3, full of ginger, black eyes sparkling as she entertained us with an ebullient flow of chatter. Suddenly, embellishing one of her little tales with a sweeping motion of her fork, she hit a goblet and shattered it. The happy little face went from smiles to instant horror.

After a session in the bedroom with her daddy, she climbed back up beside me, no longer the life of the party. I assured her that I knew it was only an accident, but her quiet sobs shuddered on beside me for some time. I felt very sorry for her and longed to gather her into my arms and say, "Forget the foolish piece of glass. Who cares?" But I respected my son's attempts to mold this little rascal into a stable young woman of the future, so I restrained my grandmotherly instincts.

Later that evening as I was putting the house back to rights, our phone rang. When I picked up the receiver, a repentant Lisa said, "I'm sorry I broke your goblet, Grandma. I'm going to work and pay for it. Goodbye." All before I had time to say a word.

Her mother told me afterward that on the way home a sad little voice from the back seat had broken the stillness. "I feel awful that I broke

Grandma's glass." Her parents had asked her if she would like to buy me a new one and told her they'd pay her for little jobs around the house until she'd saved enough. Lisa found the solution exciting (in theory, at least) and had been eager to pass the word along to me, and to restore our normal genial relationship.

As I lay in bed that night, my mind wandering idly over the events of the day, it occurred to me that Lisa's little fiasco was but a microcosm of my own long, turbulent journey with the Lord. How many times I'd felt awful about my failures to be what I want to be for Him. I hate the arid loneliness of feeling cut off from Him by my own weak tendencies to sin. Like Lisa, I long to restore the relationship, to be His friend again.

Suddenly it hit me that while Lisa had felt cut off from me I had not experienced the slightest irritation toward her. Not because I don't mind smashed dishes. That goblet, in fact, matched the china and was rather special to me. But I loved the little girl so much that her feelings meant far more to me than the glassware. But I did know that she must learn to be responsible, to curb her exuberance, and to respect the property of others. So it was necessary for me to witness her painful discipline and not to intervene.

Could it be that God never feels irritation with me? That I'm not really cut off when I sin? That though He hates the sin, His concern is centered upon my sorrow and discouragement? Yet He waits, as did I, for the Holy Spirit's discipline of conscience and repentance to do its sacred work and bring us back into harmony once more. But He's not angry or disgusted or disdainful any more than I was with little Lisa.

And another thing. Once Lisa had made things right between us—confession and plans for restitution—she hopped into bed relieved and happy. No worries about whether I would forgive. After all, I was Grandma, and Grandma is love.

You don't really need me to draw a lesson from that, do you?

The sacrifices of God are a broken spirit; a broken and contrite heart, O God, you will not despise (Ps. 51:17).

Roger Never Comes . . .

She lay curled into a fetal position, her frail, old body making only a small rise in the sterile white sheet.

"Emily," I said, "it's me—June. How are you?"

She peered at me through rheumy, unseeing eyes. "I'm not good, not good at all. I don't know you, do I? Are you going to leave me now? Please don't leave. I'm scared here. I'm scared all the time." She closed her eyes and sighed deeply. "Please don't go."

I knew it was hopeless to bring her news of the world, even the small world in which she had once lived. Everything was gone but the sightless, trembling shell that refused to die. There was little to do but hold her hand briefly until she slept.

It was hard to recognize, in the pitiful scrap before me, the vibrant woman she had once been. I remembered her best in a bright-blue coat that matched her bright-blue eyes. I had always noticed her eyes. Fringed with thick dark lashes, they'd lit her wrinkled face, reminding one she'd not always been old. I could visualize her, with her naturally curly hair, as a real beauty at 18. Even at 65 there'd been a sparkle about her, glinting like sunlight in those sea-blue eyes, that made mockery of her years.

I'd first known her widowed—but lively, independent, and well. During the passing years her health and, more cruelly, her vision had deteriorated. I'd watched her fumbling about her small house, surviving because the dim shapes were familiar and in their right places. She had a son and grandchildren, but they came less and less as she grew unable to minister and became more in need of ministry.

Finally darkness closed in, and she was bundled off to a nursing home, where she'd be "taken care of." No longer were things in their right places, so she just sat through the long days. It so happened that her son drove a bakery truck that delivered goodies to the nursing home once or twice a week. At first she awaited, with eagerness, the sound of his vehicle driving around to the back door, sure he would bound up the stairs for a brief "Good morning" and news of the grandchildren. But the welcome footsteps never came, though she could hear his loved voice below. With tears following the deep lines in her face, she had told me, "Roger never comes. He's right downstairs and he doesn't even come up." She paused, steadying her emotions. "He was always such a sweet child."

After months of sitting in the dark, the boredom broken only by an occasional visitor or phone call, she began to be confused. What day was it? Whose voice? Whose touch? The aides chided her gently. "Granny's a little mixed up today, isn't she? Why don't you watch some TV? It will help you orient yourself."

So she felt her way to the lounge and sat in front of the chattering box, which drifted from soap operas to football to soft-drink commercials that promised life. Some around her nodded. Some muttered incoherently of events long past. Others, like herself, fought to hang on to reality. But slowly it slipped away.

Today I asked her, just to make conversation, "Does Roger ever come?"

She raised her hand and peered at me through the railings of her bed. "Who is Roger?" Her querulous old voice was thin and rasping.

Her eyes took on a fierce, momentary concentration.

"Who is Roger?" Out of her long nightmare she groped for those golden moments of motherhood and then answered herself softly, "I think he was my son."

Honor your father and your mother, so that you may live long in the land the Lord your God is giving you (Ex. 20:12).

All Things Work Together . . .

The April morning was all promise and sunlight as I approached the intersection. Maples flung the red buds of springtime over the narrow side street on which I was traveling. An occasional jogger wove in and out with haughty grace among the few pedestrians. It was a good morning to be alive—or should have been.

She stood on the corner, 5 or 6 years old, crowned with two long, golden pigtails. Tears streamed down her cheeks, and the sounds of her wailing penetrated my closed car windows.

Feeling her pain and fear, I drew over to the curb while annoyed drivers behind me swerved around my vehicle. I rolled down the window and beckoned to her, well knowing that good training might force her to ignore me. But she came eagerly to the car.

"What's the trouble, sweetheart?" I scanned her round, blue-eyed face.

"I don't want to stand out here," she whimpered.

"Why are you here?"

"I'm waiting for the school bus." At the mention of the dreaded words she burst forth into fresh torrents.

"Is your mom in the house?" I asked.

She nodded gloomily. "She told me I had to go!"

"Then you do have to go, love," I said, wondering sadly what trauma in the classroom had reduced her to this state. "Cheer up. Maybe tomorrow things will look better."

What empty words! I drove away frustrated. I longed to talk with her mother and to know the real cause of this heartache. The child was neatly and attractively clad, her hair braided and tied with bright ribbons. Obviously someone cared. Quite likely her mother watched from the window, a lump in her own throat at this necessary discipline.

For a moment I had forgotten my own situation. I was facing surgery within the next few days—I who had been so gloriously healthy all my life. I felt exactly like the wailing 5-year-old. I wanted no part of it. The coward in me threatened to run off to the woods and sit down with my back against a tree, defying the prophets of doom.

I expect I feared the strange, sterile hospital atmosphere exactly as my little friend dreaded the chalky classroom. We don't really change much over the years. Only our fears change, and our ability to hide them.

I guess I'd have liked a mother, too (why do we forever want mothers when things go wrong?), but I knew that I had a Protector standing in the shadows.

That knowledge was the only thing that calmed my fears. When I felt panic rising, I said to myself, "All things work together for good to them that love God" (Rom. 8:28, KJV).

What good could possibly come from my lying under the lights with the masked men practicing their healing arts on my insides? Yet the One to whom I committed my life each morning had said—like little Miss Pigtail's mom—"You have to go."

I could go weeping and wailing, as my little friend had opted to do, or I could believe that He had His reasons—good, valid reasons, underlined with love.

Already—though I hated to admit it—I'd sensed some of those reasons. I realized how dull my ear had grown to hear His whisper, how easily I'd pushed aside His suggestions—"Later"; "Another day"—how little I'd empathized with the pains and heartaches of my fellow human beings. But now, in my own hour of need, suddenly I was made so very aware of His presence, of His willingness to communicate with me, to use me, and to comfort and nurture me.

I thought of a friend who also had recently gone through surgery.

"Are you scared?" his wife asked him as the moment approached.

"No," he replied calmly. "The Lord is my shepherd."

And though my heart may beat a bit faster when I am wheeled to the operating room, He's my Shepherd too.

And especially the little girl's on the street corner, for He loves the lambs most of all.

He will cover you with his feathers, and under his wings you will find refuge (Ps. 91:4).

My Mother-in-law's Advice

The remains of breakfast cluttered the kitchen, one unclaimed piece of toast withering on a plate. Even the brisk entrance of my mother-in-law, crisp in a fresh housedress, failed to shame me as I sat slumped in rumpled pajamas and deep depression. I, who had so longed to be a mother, had just discovered I wasn't made of the proper stuff. This fact, which had hit me along about 4:00 a.m. while floor-walking our newly adopted infant son, had left me shattered.

How would I explain to our friends that I had no idea how to cope with this wee, adorable mite who screamed endlessly with colic, that my dream of motherhood had gone no farther than a ruffled bassinet? I felt sure my nerves couldn't take one more night of lying tensely, waiting for the inevitable wail that could not be silenced with endless bottles or miles of walking. Not that I didn't love the little creature, who in rare moments of calm looked up at me with alert dark eyes. I sensed, even through my misery, that he promised delights for the future.

All this I poured into my mother-in-law's ever-sympathetic ear, while she mechanically rinsed the cereal bowls and tidied the shelves. "I'm not even sure I'll make it," I finished lamely.

Nothing in our previous relationship prepared me for her reply. "Nonsense." Without even bothering to turn from the sink, she lashed my tender immaturity. "You can go through a whole lot more than you think you can!"

Quiet descended over the kitchen while I pondered that gem. Stern and unexpected, the words challenged some reserve, some heretofore untapped strength. Maybe I could "go through."

Many years and five children later, I smile at the memory. Colic, as any experienced mother could have told me, does not last forever, and the boy who finally emerged was well worth it all. Life would have been only a fraction of joy without him. Mother was right. The human spirit is amazingly hardy.

Yet there are bleak times when one must admit the helplessness of human resources and lean hard into the strength of God. Such crises may drive a person to one's knees many times a day for that divine mending that enables one to go on.

Lately I've also come upon a different kind of situation. A friend told me recently, "I can't find God anywhere—on my knees, with the Bible, or even in church. And I've never needed Him so much. Have I somehow severed my connection with Him? Is it possible He's walked away?"

My friend was not exaggerating his troubles. He'd been buffeted from every side for a long period. I'd held my breath as he'd staggered from one heartbreak to another, wondering if my mother-in-law's old counsel would hold true in his trials. I'd comforted myself that he knew God and that with God you really can go through a whole lot more than you think you can.

Now his words startled me. So he hadn't had God after all. Well, why not? I counted him a totally honest Christian. A true seeker. If he couldn't make celestial contact in his hour of need, who could?

Then I remembered David's frantic cries in Psalm 88: "O Lord God of my salvation, I have cried day and night before thee . . . for my soul is full of troubles: and my life draweth nigh unto the grave. . . . Lord, I have called daily upon thee, I have stretched out my hands unto thee. . . . Lord, why casteth thou off my soul? why hidest thou thy face from me?" (verses 1-14, KJV).

Had God rejected David? By no means. David was a favorite of His. Yet David felt the same alienation that my friend was experiencing. Can it be that God tests those who reach out to Him most ardently by stepping into the shadows temporarily? Will they hold fast? Will they trust His presence even when they have no awareness of it? Can they, putting their faith in His character and His promises, move forward through pain and disaster in calm trust?

Maybe when God appears to turn His face away, it's our most crucial hour, our ultimate testing.

"Just hold on," I said to my friend. "You're very special to God, and you can go through a whole lot more than you think you can."

Be still before the Lord and wait patiently for him; do not fret (Ps. 37:7).

The Garage-Sale Zither

Years ago, when she was only a child, we took our oldest daughter to a Deutschmeister concert in the city of Buffalo. There were bright costumes and very lively marches, and all in all it was a delightful and most unusual evening. We agreed, on the way home, that the zither solo was the high point of the program.

Later we purchased some zither recordings and played them occasionally when we felt nostalgic for that pleasant evening. But the girl grew up, and our musical tastes changed, and the records were relegated to the attic.

In the long process of rearing six children and launching a writing career, I had little time to think of zithers or any other frivolity, for that matter. Probably it would have remained that way had it not been for the garage sale. I was poking about among old magazines, cheap glass pieces, secondhand clothing, and tacky lamps (wishing I had never come), when I saw it sitting under a table leaned up against a box of worse-for-wear toys. A zither. An honest-to-goodness old, old zither. I'm not an impulsive buyer, but I knew that was one item I'd not go home without. We did a little bargaining, the owner and I, and $40 poorer, I walked toward my car with the zither.

He told me he'd bought it in the Adirondacks years before, meaning to repair and play it, as he and his sons were guitar enthusiasts and thus familiar with stringed instruments. But, as so often happens, his initial enthusiasm waned, and it found its way to the attic. Supposedly he'd paid $50 for it, and I was getting a great bargain, as it was much closer to becoming an antique than when he purchased it.

As an old auction/flea market addict, I took it all with a grain of salt, but I wasn't buying it as an investment anyhow. I had quite simply fallen in love with it. No matter that it had a bad crack or two and was missing 13 of its 100 strings (or so the owner informed me). It had a Victorian looking rose decal beneath the words "Hopf's Jubelklange" and a lovely harplike shape.

Right now it's leaned up against the fireplace, and the grandchildren like to pluck the horribly untuned strings as they pass by. Our antique-collecting friends think it's an interesting piece (if not exactly vintage), and music lovers urge me to have it repaired. That's my dream. To clean the dirty old wood, and have the cracks filled and the missing strings replaced.

I long to hear some expert hand draw a simple tune from my

garage-sale gem. Perhaps by the time I arrive at that place, I'll have invested enough to have bought a brand-new zither, but somehow I prefer restoring the old one.

It's given me some insights into the restoration going on in my own life. That zither is totally dependent upon me for repairs. If I choose to ignore it, it will sit upon my hearth in its shabby state forever, but because I'm fond of it, I shall go to great lengths to make it like new again.

There is One who, for the same reason, is mending my life with infinite care. There are gaping cracks in my character, and the fruit of the Spirit is far from complete in me. My life is still sadly discordant, but He has promised to make me new, a harmonious creature in the end. I can only trust to His loving concern for me. I can do no more about my deterioration than can the dusty zither, but how fortunate we both are to have someone committed to our restoration.

Here the parallel breaks down, however, for I have the capacity for gratitude. The zither doesn't. And, oh, am I grateful!

> Throughout eternity, God willing,
> My life shall be a hymn of praise
> To Him whose pledged and patient mending
> Fills these earthly days.

Look to the Lord and his strength; seek his face always (1 Chron. 16:11).

There Will Always Be Children

Our local symphony orchestra advertised a youth concert spotlighting the talents of the most musically gifted children and teens in our area. Using my approaching birthday as leverage, I wheedled my husband into purchasing tickets. We were joined by two friends and settled into our seats with anticipation.

I love the preconcert rustle of programs and muted conversation. To my delight, nearly every other number on the program was performed by an Asian child. (It so happens we have a number of Oriental doctors in our city, and evidently their offspring are both ambitious and talented.) Because we had reared two Korean children and an Aleut in our own home, those golden-skinned youngsters with their serious, tilted dark eyes had special appeal for us. Asian children have a grace, a delicate beauty, that cannot be duplicated. Interspersed among them were handsome youth of strictly American heritage. We were hard put to choose between the tiny 4-year-old Korean who could barely make it onto the piano bench and the fair-skinned Yankee fiddler who rendered a lively "Fiddle-Faddle."

At some point in the program I realized I was experiencing a deep, mysterious satisfaction. During an especially long piano number I tried to analyze what was making me feel so good. The youngsters were giving us our money's worth, no doubt about that, but it was something more. An old, familiar pleasure out of the past. Something that felt terribly comfortable and relaxing, like a Pendleton suit one has worn for 12 years. Whatever it was, I had to define it and somehow retain it.

A lovely Oriental child, maybe 7 or 8, took her place with violin. Her straight dark hair was pulled neatly back into a ponytail, and her sober, inscrutable eyes assessed the audience as she waited out her accompanist's introduction.

Suddenly I knew the answer. It wasn't the music (though it had been excellent) that had been bringing me those good vibes. It was the children themselves. Our home, now so bereft after 25 years of youthful antics, was neat, dull, and quiet. I missed youth's fresh thinking, its humor, its sense of adventure. Its originality. Its kindness. I missed silly conversations and spontaneous expressions of love. I missed the wit of teenagers and their wry, wise appraisals of life.

Here in this auditorium I was, for a brief moment, enriched once more with the uniqueness of the young. No matter that they were other people's children. It detracted not one whit from my pleasure. In fact, having no child of my own on the program, I could relax and simply enjoy, without that mix of terror and pride that one experiences when one's own child is about to perform.

There would always be children. Why hadn't I realized that? I had only to seek them out. Some I could observe, as I was doing today. Others I could befriend. Some I could help. Shy children, who needed someone to stoop down and converse at their level in a quiet voice. Children whose world was cracking and heaving beneath them, who needed a loving touch and a reassuring word. Children who were hungry and whose clothes were cheap and threadbare. I could make a difference in their lives. I must watch for them, even search for them.

There would always be healthy, handsome, loved children who would make me glad simply by their existing. The little boy in church who gives me a friendly whack as he goes by or who waves his jacket arms at me in an "amputated" way as he grins mischievously. Or my little friend Renee, who looks at me with the biggest, brownest eyes I've ever seen and wraps me in her slow, sweet, mysterious smile.

The Korean lassie pulled the bow across the strings in a delicate, precise finale, bowed with unhurried grace, and left the stage. I joined in the applause with a light heart. I did not need to fear her departure or the end of the program. There will always be children, and ways in which you and I can enrich their lives. It's a ministry in which Christ joyously joins us. He has a special place in His heart for the little members of his Earth family.

And he took the children in his arms, put his hands on them and blessed them (Mark 10:16).

End of the Fairy Tales

Recently I had opportunity to mingle with a group of old school friends whom I had not seen for many a year. Nearly 40 springs had come and gone since we'd studied, worked, and played together. We'd all been so eager then, confident that life would be a piece of cake for the likes of us.

But the years, as they have a way of doing, cuffed us around a bit. Divorce ripped through some homes like a tornado, leaving loneliness and shattered children in its wake. No one had risen to fame, though some had done well. Most of us were living ordinary lives, surprised and a little uneasy that the years had slipped away so quickly. We talked about old dreams, old romances, old pranks, old teachers, and wandered briefly throughout sunlit youths. We talked about our children, the ones who'd made us proud and the ones who'd broken our hearts.

Mary (that's not her real name, of course) had been the star of her class. Nothing but a straight 4.0. Now she stood before me, sorrow softening her dark eyes. "My marriage was a mistake from the first day," she said. "It's been a nightmare hanging on and being faithful all these years, but the Lord has sustained."

"Do you have children?" I asked.

"A few." A spark of mischief flickered through the sadness.

"Like how many?"

"Like nine." She chuckled at my astonishment. "Right now I'm working two jobs to keep the youngest in academy. He's a handsome boy." There was pride in her voice.

110

"Somehow I wonder if I know the Lord," she mused, "as it's possible to know Him. When you were never close to your father and then your marriage is a bummer too, it's hard to find a relationship with God. You think there's just something hopelessly wrong with you that will forever close the doors to love, even divine love. I never even had a real friend in school."

"I guess we all thought you didn't need anyone up there in those lofty academic realms," I defended lamely.

"I was so lonely," she said quietly, without accusation, "but now I just want to know God loves me. I want to feel it personally in my heart. I think I could bear everything else if I could just get hold of that."

"Oh, He does love you, Mary," I assured, "but, I too have had trouble at times accepting that love personally. Let's pray for each other." If only I'd known.

Laura sat on my bed and pulled funny stories out of the past. We laughed and marveled that we'd ever been so young and giddy.

"Where do you live?" I asked.

"Out in the boonies in an ancient house. When I bought it, they said it had a space heater, and I thought that was something new from NASA."

She grinned.

"I found out a lot of things about that house after I'd lived in it a few months."

"Are you alone?" This girl had been so merry, so outgoing. Surely she'd found some kind and caring man.

"I married a man with lots of money. He was really going places. We had a cottage on the ocean, and I spent a lot of time there in the summers with our little boy. Too much time, I guess, because once while I was gone he found someone else." She shrugged it off lightly. "It was all a long time ago. Since then Billy and I've been on our own. I put on my nursing cap and we've survived, but it's not easy raising a teenage kid alone."

"I don't see how you've done it," I said, almost ashamed of the love and security within my own home.

"One day at a time, with my hand in the Lord's," she answered soberly. We hugged each other, and she went out into the summer night, the carefree long ago intermingling with present stern realities.

I lay awake awhile that night and thought of Mary and Laura, and lifted them up to God. I concluded (1) that one's choice of a marriage partner is so crucial a decision that it must never be made without much prayer and counsel, and (2) that God is holding a lot of lives together on this sad old planet. I hope He'll let us help, you and me, whenever He can.

Be strong and courageous. Do not be terrified; do not be discouraged, for the Lord your God will be with you wherever you go (Joshua 1:9).

Seeking the Ultimate Friendship

A friend called this morning—a new friend. Last spring at the Greater New York Women's Prayer Retreat I was assigned a prayer partner. Sometimes, as the speaker, I do not get a prayer partner, but Greater New York is into prayer, and they're wise enough to know that often the speaker is in more need of intercession than anyone else.

Veda turned out to be a Black woman somewhere in the vicinity of my own age. Before she ever spoke a word, I knew I had lucked out. She looked steady and patient and kind. I am a high-strung worrier and sensed immediately I'd have much to learn from this woman. Besides that, I felt very comfortable with her, as though we were just continuing an old conversation.

Our lives have been quite different. Veda raised her two children alone, against a lot of odds, and quite splendidly I might add. Today they are young adults, successful in their chosen careers. When cast upon her own resources as a young mother, she went back to school and became an RN, providing herself with a profession and means of support for her children. I wonder what I would have done under the same circumstances. I'm sure the strength she radiates today developed, to a great degree, from her day-by-day dependence upon God during those early years.

My time of hardship came much earlier in life than hers and was of a totally different nature, but we both know the meaning of trouble and heartache.

We've both made our peace with the past, and are living happy, well-adjusted lives today. We are each active in our local churches. I'm a writer, and she works with struggling addicts in a hospital rehab unit. God has given us interesting careers.

So when I heard her gentle voice on the phone this morning, it was with deepest pleasure that I sat down at the dining table to chat and eventually to pray.

What a priceless gift a friend is, especially a praying friend, a follower of Christ! We acquire a lot of friends during a lifetime. They range from little more than acquaintances to deep, complex, long-term relationships that enrich us to the very end. Usually the latter type can be counted upon one hand.

Dr. Theodore I. Rubin, famed psychoanalyst, once wrote: "We demonstrate our emotional health or sickness through our friends, or our lack of them. One of the key questions in a psychological mental examination is: Have you had any sustained relationships? A 'yes' answer immediately assures the examiner that the patient probably has considerable mental health. Long-term happy friendships indicate that a person has a strong sense of self-worth and the feelings and ability to give of him or herself without the fear of becoming depleted. People without friends are usually emotionally disturbed, withdrawn, and seclusive."

So I am grateful to those women who have added a dimension to my life besides mother, wife, and daughter. Childhood friends, academy and college friends, and those gems stumbled upon throughout adulthood.

What of friendship with God? Moses said the Lord spoke to him face-to-face, as a man speaks with his friend (Ex. 33:11). Is that kind of experience available to us in 1993? Probably most of us would chorus yes. We as Christians know the right answers. But I think about my friendship with Nina. It's old and steady and a great source of joy and security. I am never afraid to tell her anything, even about the worst ugliness of my character, my failures, and my disappointments.

I do not fear she will reject me, nor forget me. Ever. There is no fear in our relationship.

Sometimes I am a bit afraid of God—not because He's cruel or vindictive, but because I'm very aware of my sins. The problem is mine, not His. I know that I cannot be a friend of the world and His friend too (James 4:4). So in that respect my friendship with Nina is more comfortable. She's in this struggle with me.

But there's another factor to consider. When I share my sins with Nina, she can only encourage. She cannot deliver. But God can. And does. He doesn't want me to be afraid. As my shaky faith becomes more constant and strong, I have a friendship with God superseding all others. At this point He can effect radical change in my life.

So my daily prayer is for a faith that overrides fear, a perfect trust that frees me for perfect friendship with God, the kind Moses had.

I wish that for you, too!

Two are better than one. . . . : If one falls down, his friend can help him up (Eccl. 4: 9, 10).

Observations From an Eagle's Nest

Seated here on a little balcony clinging to the nineteenth floor of a Boston hotel, I survey the glittering city spread out before me. Across the way a great neon sign spells BRADFORD against the night sky. In the distance I can see the lights of Fenway Park, where my family are watching the Red Sox play.

Today a fellow guest pointed out to us, as we looked down upon the city, a section below that was not safe for pedestrians at night. Soberly he cautioned us to avoid the area. Now, hearing sirens, I watch from my secure and lofty perch as a police car noses down its dark alleys upon some murky mission.

When I opted not to attend the ball game, I had planned to read, but should have known better. I can never concentrate in a hotel room. I do not like hotel rooms. Better to sleep in a friendly corn patch. Well, almost. So I have decided to give my head a vacation and let my thoughts run willy-nilly.

I ponder the past and the present of this sprawling old metropolis, which even in its infancy elbowed its way into the world of commerce with proud clipper ships gracing its harbor.

If fiery Sam Adams were to return to life, he could still locate familiar landmarks. Just today I strolled in the Boston Commons, which he knew as a grazing ground for cattle and sheep. I saw beer cans and two policemen discouraging a street fight. That might have startled Sam a bit, although I guess anyone who was involved in the Boston Tea Party wouldn't blanch at a little skirmish. Just a couple of aimless young toughs with nothing better to do than hurl insults at each other. The officers' motorcycles throbbed a patient backdrop for the rise and fall of angry voices. The crowd soon lost interest and drifted away. At least the Tea Party had purpose.

I have never lived in a city—oh, briefly once or twice in very small ones, but never in one of these great snarling, shoving, glistening, wonderful, awful places. Occasionally our family spends a vacation week in some distant city as a refreshing contrast to our normal pastoral surroundings. It's our two youngest, 16 and 20, the only ones summering at home, who put the pressure on.

I suppose Don and I would lounge on our shady front lawn with a stack of books if given our druthers. But once we are whirled into the mad pace of urban life, we find our imaginations captured by its eclectic fare, and we're glad we came. Wouldn't have missed Quincy Market for the world. Shells and chic apparel. Salads and brimming bowls of chopped fresh fruit. Posters and fudge. Art and bagels. Crafts and tacos. Crepes and flowers.

It's absolutely my favorite place in all of Boston. Better than the harbor or the glass flowers at Cambridge or Bunker Hill or the Commons. It's a place of life and color and vitality.

Amy and I discuss what we shall take home to remind us of this sunny morning, with the gulls and the smell of the sea about us. I choose a poster done in watercolors of Faneuil Hall and the marketplace, seeing already how fine it will look against the mellow old wood of my office walls. Amy selects some postcards, and we both indulge in one of those huge cups of fresh fruit.

Don and Mitch, not so enchanted as we, are listening to the uninhibited patter of a young man broadcasting live from a van parked in the midst of the confusion. This is much more to their liking.

But that was hours ago, and now the marketplace is still, and I am alone. The city is lovely in its evening dress, but I know that out there in the velvet blackness, studded with light, men and women weep. That some moan in pain. That they lie in gutters and stagger down littered alleys. That little children whimper in their sleep, and that the young break their tender skin with needles. That even the lovely old homes harbor crumbling marriages and bitter accusations—and secret fears.

What has happened to us, this race rooted in Eden? We who can create Empire State Buildings and Golden Gate Bridges and Boeing 747s but cannot rule our own souls? Here amid the streetlights and freeways we are sick with the cancer of sin. Yet One who never sleeps bends low to heal and mend. To country and city dweller alike, His voice calls softly in the night. I pray, here on my borrowed balcony, that we all will reach out and be made whole.

For the Son of Man came to seek and to save what was lost (Luke 19:10).

Loneliness, Love Songs, and a Cross

As I went about the kitchen cleanup operation, somewhere in the distance—probably from an offspring's bedroom—came a medley of country music. I wasn't really listening, or thought I wasn't, until I realized tears were stinging my eyes. Now, I'm not one to weep over the ballads of Kenny Rogers. So I really tuned in to the lyrics and realized the vocalist was singing an oldie:

"Come sit by my side, little darlin';
Do not hasten to bid me adieu."

Now I understood the tears . . . and shed some more. Thirty-five years before, my grandmother had died, leaving my grandfather and me (I had been raised in their home) to fend for ourselves. Because she'd been a very nurturing person, we weren't much good at our new assignment. Somehow Sundays were the worst. I'm not sure why. Perhaps because that was the only day Gramp allowed himself any respite from a grueling work schedule.

So on those long-ago Sundays, when he could no longer stand the quiet house, he'd sometimes get two tin pails off the shelf and announce that we were going berrying.

Because his work took him all around the county, he knew where sturdy raspberry canes shot up out of old cellar holes and along overgrown back roads. At 16 I didn't rate raspberry picking very high on my list of favorite activities, but there wasn't much else to do out there in the mountains of Vermont, so off we went.

After robbing the bushes of their sweet red fruit for a sun-warmed hour or so, we'd get back into the car and wander over some of the most remote areas in the region—staving off that hour when we must go home.

We didn't talk much, but Gramp sang. Looking back, I expect he had a pretty good voice. By nature he was a rather stern, silent man, but he often sang. On those Sunday afternoons he started off with hymns, though he never pretended to be on speaking terms with God. Then he'd ease into "Sweetheart of the Rockies." I felt almost an intruder, but understood that he needed me there with him. The hurt was too much to bear alone. We'd ride on and on through the desolate beauty of those mountains in the summer dusk with only my grandfather's plaintive singing breaking the stillness.

And now the stereo was playing "Come sit by my side . . ." and I was torn apart with loneliness and angry with all that humanity has suffered over the centuries. I wanted to hear my grandfather's voice again and reach out and touch his worn and weathered hands, long laid to rest.

I was angry with death, which had invaded my life too many times. Angry for a friend who has cancer and who must live from week to week hoping that radiation will hold the enemy at bay. Even before I ask, I can tell by his eyes which way the battle is going. Normally they are laughing, mischievous eyes, but of late they are often sad.

I was angry for a 16-year-old girl who'd overdosed and whose screams had echoed all night throughout hospital corridors. I wanted out of this nightmare we call life. I was overcome with sadness, a deep hurt that penetrated every corner of my inner self. All the atrocities I'd borne with admirable stoicism throughout life suddenly assaulted me with unbearable clarity. And what was my pain in comparison with the accumulated pain of the ages—or even the daily pain of the small city in which I live?

And where could we hide, we battered, defenseless humans? Where could we run? There is no city of refuge for the victims of Satan's tyranny.

Or is there? I glimpse the shadow of a cross stretching over the earth. A cross where Another wrestled pain and death to the ground through an agony worse than you or I will ever know. I run to the safety of that shadow, knowing it cannot erase my past pain, nor can it afford me immunity from future pain, until its Victim returns in triumph for those who've put their trust in Him. He'll find them all beneath that cross. I intend to be there. How about you?

Then Pilate took Jesus and had him flogged. The soldiers twisted together a crown of thorns and put it on his head. They clothed him in a purple robe and went up to him again and again, saying, "Hail, king of the Jews!" And they struck him in the face (John 19:1-3).

Celebrities—Divine and Otherwise

R obert Redford came to Stafford, New York, in August of 1983. I know because I live in a neighboring town that stirred slightly in the backwash of this unusual event. Unusual because Stafford is one of those charming but obscure little villages scattered throughout our end of New York State. You know the kind—a few gracious old homes, a general store, a town hall, a church or two. Not the kind of place where stars of Redford's caliber usually make appearances.

But it seems that in one of his upcoming movies a locale was needed simulating that of Nebraska, and here in the little town of Stafford they found a run-down farmhouse with an adjoining field of golden wheat, ripe for the harvest. Just what they'd been looking for.

Also, they needed a boy to play Redford as a child. So the local sons lined up, each hoping for his moment of glory in an honest-to-goodness film. The chosen child was ultimately dressed up in a plaid shirt and overalls and directed about in the front yard of the old house until his performance became convincing. Exciting days for small-town America.

But of course, the main attraction was the arrival of the star himself. On the appointed day eager fans lined both sides of the street down which his car would pass. Waiting in the hot summer sun, they bore welcoming banners and discussed this unique opportunity that was theirs. "Imagine seeing him in person," sighed one. "Perhaps when he sees us he'll stop and shake hands." "Or even just wave and flash that famous smile at us," said another hopefully.

But alas, when the illustrious cavalcade rolled into town, the long-awaited star crouched into his seat, hiding himself from his would-be admirers.

They straggled home, the residents of Stafford, disillusioned, disappointed, their banners trailing. The glittering moment had turned to tinsel, or maybe even tinfoil.

Later others, with binoculars, watched the filming from a half mile away and muttered, "There, I think *that's* him. The one in the blue shirt coming down the steps."

"Naw, that's just one of the crew. I bet Redford's the one in the T-shirt."

But they never really knew, for the object of their adulation was too far away, his privacy closely guarded.

This is not written to belittle Robert Redford. Perhaps one grows weary, even scornful, of the fawning masses. Surely he had his reasons.

But after the celebrity had moved on and the wheatfield was once again just an ordinary New York cash crop, I thought about the people, those who had gone out to meet him. They were no different from people everywhere.

We ache to break the monotony of our lives with something new. Something lighter, brighter, more fanciful than our mundane selves. In each of us there's a desire to worship and emulate.

Sometimes, sadly, we worship and emulate each other. We look to the Robert Redfords of this world to give us brief moments of fantasy, forgetting that they, like us, know loneliness, fear, and pain.

I wondered, on that day of Stafford's disappointment, why we are so slow to understand that only Jesus fills the void within our hearts. Even if Robert Redford had stopped and dispensed hugs and handshakes all around, the moment would have passed, and the citizens would have returned home no better or no worse. Perhaps a little lonelier, with the object of their admiration soon fading into distant memory.

But it's not like that with Jesus. He comes with the dignity of royalty, yet bearing an equal and constant love for all. He chooses not only the witty, the wise, and the beautiful. For He sees each one of us as a potentially attractive, intelligent, interesting being. He sees what we can become through association with Him, and He loves us as though we are already that way.

He never grows weary of our needs and withdraws. He never crouches in the seat, for there's no welcome He loves more than that from those He died to save. Look carefully. Is He not more worthy of your adoration than the citizens of Hollywood?

Whom do we worship, you and I, while the Prince of heaven passes by?

Do not be overawed when a man grows rich, . . . for he will take nothing with him when he dies (Ps. 49:16, 17).

Clap your hands, all you nations; shout to God with cries of joy. How awesome is the Lord Most High, the great King over all the earth! (Ps. 47:1, 2).

Harder Than I Thought

It's hard to be a follower of Jesus Christ. Exciting; many moments of holy joy, yes—but so very difficult at times. On many occasions the Jesus-way slips over my sinner's skin like a scratchy wool sweater. I love the sweater. I long to be comfortable in it and have made a commitment to adapt to it. But there are times I feel like ripping it off and giving up on it.

I never will, though, because 45 years ago I caught the vision of the Jesus way. It seemed to come so naturally to Him—the gentleness, the compassion, the wisdom, the unselfishness. I want to be like that too. I want to evidence my loyalty to Him by obedience. I want to leave a trail of joy and healing behind me as He did. I understand that His way represents a new and genuine happiness which is foreign to Planet Earth.

Yet my definition of happiness, the undisciplined sinner's happiness, often screams for attention. It's then that I long to fling the scratchy garment aside, and just relax and bow to the control of my fallen state. Sadly, sometimes I do, but our gracious Saviour has made provision for even such failures, through His death upon the cross.

When I first fell in love with Christ, it seemed it would be easy. It took me a long time to realize I was wrong. No matter how determinedly I'd set my will, some ugly force within would topple all my best intentions. It was frustrating and discouraging. Why couldn't I be like the apostle Paul, who cheerfully faced beatings, stonings, imprisonment, and shipwreck?

Then one day I came upon this quotation: "Paul's sanctification was a constant conflict with self. Said he: 'I die daily.' *His will and his desires every day conflicted with duty and the will of God.* Instead of following inclination, he did the will of God, however unpleasant and crucifying to his nature" (*Testimonies*, vol. 4, p. 299; italics supplied).

Well! What an insight! It was hard for Paul, too. "Crucifying to his nature." "Unpleasant." But day by day he subjected his will to the shining glory of the One he'd glimpsed on the road to Damascus. And he admitted it was death to the comfortable old life every morning.

A costly venture, this narrow path to the kingdom. An impossible assignment without strength from an Outside Source.

Why do we bother, we His followers? Why was Paul willing to "die" every morning? Is it only because we fear eternal loss, the displeasure of God, the fires of hell?

Somehow, I don't think so. Deep within each of us there's a memory of the sweetness of Eden. The innocence, the purity, the one-on-one friendship with God. No ambivalence, no confusion, no tug-of-war between the powers of good and evil within us day and night. Just perfect peace, harmony with the universe, and a constant awareness of God's pleasure in us. We ache to find our way back to that, and a "scratchy sweater" is a small price to pay.

There are moments when it all clicks in. Sometimes I read a verse of Scripture and glimpse a concept so far beyond my normal, mundane, muddled ponderings that something in me responds at a deep, deep level. I know then that I'm a child of God, lost, it's true, in a dangerous and alien land, but nevertheless of royal lineage. I know then why Paul was willing to die daily and why I don't cast off the scratchy sweater. We're both addicted to freedom, a freedom sweet and singing, elusive as a soap bubble, but ours, truly ours, if we are willing to let go of old things and old ways.

Come join me. Don't flinch at the pain of rebirth. Keep your eyes on Jesus and your feet on the narrow path.

Those who live according to the sinful nature have their minds set on what that nature desires; but those who live in accordance with the Spirit have their minds set on what the Spirit desires (Rom. 8:5).

Become Menders, Not Renders

Lynda Fisher greeted her guest with warmth and anticipation. She liked the older woman and looked forward to her visits. They sat together at the kitchen table as they sipped cinnamon-apple tea and chatted about Lynda's small children and Esther's grown ones, their church and its activities, and the recent heavy rains on the southern California coast.

At some point Esther's expression changed, and her voice lowered. "Lynda, you will not believe what I heard about Kathy Mason the other day. My source is absolutely dependable. It seems that Kathy was once in trouble with . . ."

My young friend Lynda raised her small, neatly manicured hand. "Esther, I don't want to hear another word. Not one. What can possibly be gained by you and me discussing Kathy's past? I have felt the bitter lash of gossip in my own life, and I have determined never to inflict that kind of pain on anyone else."

Though Lynda tried to turn the conversation to other topics, Esther soon took her leave. Lynda realized that their friendship might never be quite the same again. She wonders if she could have handled the situation in some more tactful way, but she has no regrets about refusing to dissect verbally a mutual acquaintance.

This little episode reminded me of Solomon's words: "The tongue has the power of life and death" (Prov. 18:21). I wondered how many times I had destroyed with words. I fear that we all tend to flit gleefully, like venomous butterflies, from friend to friend with our lethal messages.

And, oh, how we rationalize that the story must be told. We mask the tales with sorrowful faces and declarations of pity for the victim. Or we take a righteous stance, like the moralists of old who dragged their prey to the feet of Jesus for retribution. It has been said that what Jesus wrote upon the ground were the sins of her accusers. If so, there's a subtle lesson there for us. While we are whispering the failings and shortcomings of others, I expect that to the astute observer, our own lack of love and compassion lights up like a neon sign.

I once had a friend who never gossiped. This characteristic of her conversation was so obvious that I was never even slightly tempted to discuss individuals with her. I have no idea how she would have handled it had I stooped to slander, but I do know we spent delightful hours together discussing natural science (which was her bag), literature (which was mine), children (of which we both had too many, in the opinion of others), and the Bible (which was the taproot of our strength for all that mothering).

We have been apart for many years and our children are all young adults, but I still miss the keen clicking of our minds as our offspring romped the green lawns (and got into mischief) while we pondered the wonders of nature and the words of God and humanity.

As Christian women, I hope we do not betray others by so much as a glance or a lift of an eyebrow. If some tantalizing morsel of gossip trembles upon our lips, let us remember Lynda's upraised hand and become menders rather than renders.

The lips of the righteous know what is fitting, but the mouth of the wicked only what is perverse (Prov. 10:32).

Gift From a Teenager

Though I looked reasonably presentable on the outside, I arrived on my hostess's doorstep in a state of mental disarray. In fact, that seems to be a rather chronic condition with me lately. My mind bubbles with lists of unfulfilled tasks, projects still in the planning stage, plots for books that never materialize, concerns for our children, and on and on.

But this evening Eunie had invited a group of old friends for a summer picnic on her breezeway, and I welcomed the outing as a respite from the frantic scurryings of my days.

Around card tables we ate salads and caught up on the news since last we'd met. We were a group of writers, but we didn't talk shop in the beginning, not while we ate. We talked about sons and daughters soon to enter second grade and college, for we were all ages. We talked about vacations and weddings. About food and whether the nasturtiums decorating the deviled eggs were edible.

Across from me sat Shirley in a lacy white blouse and gathered denim skirt—the kind of outfit my daughters wear. There's a sweet graciousness about this young woman that springs, I've always felt, from her Christianity. Somehow she seems to have escaped the pressured pace.

"How's your summer been?" she asked, sipping punch and shivering a little in the early evening breeze.

"Hectic," I replied. "Some really nice things have been happening, but I can't seem to slow down long enough to savor them."

"That's exactly how I feel," she said, a little startled (as though she'd glanced into a mirror). "So many demands on my time. Mostly things I enjoy doing, but too many of them. I try to slow down, but can never quite pull it off."

So her calm demeanor only masked a frustration not unlike my own! I had a feeling that if we had taken a poll, we'd have found it a chronic affliction in the group—in the world, for that matter. We have somehow lost leisure.

After a tour of Eunie's gardens, we adjourned to her living room, where she announced that before we settled into the business of the evening, her son would perform on the piano for us. Now Steve is a teenager and a very talented one. We knew we were in for a treat. With a delightful lack of self-consciousness—a sort of "I'm doing this for Mom" attitude that would have been very appealing even if he had been merely a mediocre pianist, he sat down at the piano. But when Steve's young fingers touch the keys, one dismisses the word "mediocre." He's good.

I didn't recognize the melody, but it was lovely and somehow eased my hurried and harassed soul into something close to peace. I sensed it was possible to live forever in a moment. To drink deeply and derive nourishment for all the barren places, past and future.

I looked about at my fellow scribblers, realizing how rich I was in friendship. We'd shared more than manuscripts. We'd lived a large hunk of life side by side. Rejoicing together. Sorrowing together. Creating together.

Steve had enabled me to experience at a deeper level. To feel the sweetness of relationships blended with an almost sensuous joy in the music. I was not giving anything. Nor doing anything. Nor planning anything. I was taking. Taking healing from a teenager who didn't even know he was giving. Nor did he know how exquisite was his gift. Nor how needed. Thank you, Steve.

Therefore encourage one another and build each other up (1 Thess. 5:11).

You Won't Forget Us, Will You?

Our oldest son, his wife, and their 3-year-old daughter were heading west. Not in a covered wagon, but in a thrifty little Subaru. They weren't going on a vacation. They were going to stay. To seek their fortune in the rolling hills of eastern Washington. They were leaving at night, and that made it worse. Everything is worse at night.

We had said goodbye to this boy many times. He'd been away to summer camps, boarding academy, various adventures in his premarriage days, but this was different. Always before, we knew he'd be home, sooner or later. This time we had an uneasy feeling that it was a permanent move.

He spread out the map on our dining room table and showed his father the route he'd charted with a red marking pen across mountains and deserts. I noticed the slightest tremor in his hand as it moved over the map.

It was nothing, of course. People switch coasts every day. But there was a heaviness resting upon us, his father and me. Concern for their safety—and something more. Something hard to define. A kind of ruthless surgery of the heart one experiences when children cut the very last home tie and strike out on their own. We sensed a sadness in him too. Breaking away from all that's familiar and dear isn't easy for children, either. Only tiny Jenny looked upon the whole thing as a great adventure.

"Grandma, we're going to see Dan and Sherry [friends with whom they would stay until they found work].

"Daddy made me a little bed in the back of the car, where I can look up at the stars.

"Promise me you'll come see us in the spring. Come on, promise now."

We talked of mileage and daily destinations, avoiding the moment of parting. My husband tucked money into our son's shirt pocket, and I slipped a few bills to his wife "for an emergency"—as parents have done over the years. It made us feel better (and undoubtedly them, too), but nothing took away the pain of saying goodbye.

We moved out to their car, and Jenny showed us, amid the jumble of all their earthly possessions, the little nest that was hers beneath the large rear window. Here, well padded with quilts and surrounded with toys, she'd watch America unroll behind her. She had no comprehension of her precarious future. She knew only that, somehow, those two adults she trusted would provide for her. Hugging a favorite doll under one arm, with simple faith she gave us each a kiss and climbed into her makeshift bed. As I tucked her blanket around her I sent up a little prayer that the angels would guard her carefully.

We lingered in the driveway, and I could see our son storing his mind with the familiar sights and sounds about him, all softened with the darkness of the warm summer night. The huge red barn, scene of so many childhood adventures, the waterfall music of the stream falling into the pond, the rolling green lawns he'd mowed so many times, and the old white farmhouse that harbored the hurts and happinesses of growing up. I understood his reluctance to leave it all behind. I also understood the need to venture forth and try a new life in a new place with his new family.

When we had hugged all around and none of us could speak, they got into the car. Don and I had turned to go inside when we realized that the car had stopped and our son had turned to speak once more. Very carefully, because his voice still was not steady, he said, "You won't forget us, will you?"

We could only shake our heads in mute assurance, and I no longer fought the tears that rolled down my cheeks. But in that moment I learned an infinitely valuable lesson. The possibility of our forgetting our oldest son was so ridiculous that I would have smiled had the moment not been so tender. He was engraved upon our hearts. No amount of time or distance could ever change that.

I caught a glimpse, then, as the small car's taillights disappeared into the night, of God's love for me. Could it be that I was so engraved upon His heart that no measure of distance or time could diminish His caring and concern? Never before had that fact been reality for me, until in my own parental sorrow I felt my heavenly Father's unchanging, unmerited love for me. God used a painful goodbye to show me something about Himself and our relationship. I hope I can hang on to it.

How great is the love the Father has lavished on us, that we should be called children of God! (1 John 3:1).

Meet My Friend Nina

You probably have one friend who stands out above all others. So do I. Her name is Nina, and we've shared so many problems, heartaches, and joys that we almost know what the other is thinking before she speaks.

At one point in our lives we were separated by hundreds of miles and we had to depend on the mail carrier and the phone to keep our friendship intact. During that period she wrote me a letter in which she shared the following experience. It touched my heart and will yours also, I'm sure.

"As I walked into his living room, I was somewhat surprised at the tidiness. It was the dark finger marks located strategically on the doorframes and on the walls that reminded me the blind must always be organized and know exactly where everything is placed. His bedroom and living room, at quick glance, gave the appearance of a fastidious woman's arranging, except for the layers of dust and a dirty carpet. And that's the reason I had come.

"I quickly vacuumed and dusted and attempted to wash walls. I then moved into the kitchen and, startled at the scene, was sorry at once I had spent so much time in the other two rooms. Grease spatterings on the entire stove and cabinet fronts had collected dust and dirt for years. Several hours, several layers of skin, and a large can of scouring powder later, I proceeded to the bathroom.

"The combination of my sore hands, weariness, and that bathroom made me want to run away crying like a little girl. But after collecting myself, I went out to purchase some bathroom cleaner and rubber gloves.

"Every public rest room across America would have to take second place to that stool. Even the walls were spattered with several years' buildup of urine.

"At long last it was clean. Then I sat and chatted with him. He had just come from the hospital and couldn't stop bubbling with excitement about the wonderful food he had been served there. I asked him how he managed to cook for himself, and he said he could prepare TV dinners, potpies, and boiled eggs. His family had left him, and he knew nothing of their whereabouts. His pension for the blind amounted to $245 a month, of which half went for rent. He couldn't afford to buy himself as much as a necktie, and never indulged in the luxury of baked goods or desserts.

"As I left, he said, 'Thank you, girlie' in a rather offhanded manner. 'Thank you, girlie,' indeed! I glanced at my raw hands, while a little flame of indignation flickered within. I guess I thought I had earned the Congressional Medal of Honor!

"It wasn't until driving home that I realized why there had been no fanfare over what I had done. He couldn't see his black dishcloth or his bathroom crawling with germs. Neither could he see the changes I had wrought. How could it really matter to him? His courage for living, and confidence that the Lord would provide his daily bread, shamed my ugly need for gratitude.

"With a new awareness of my own blessings, I told God I would gladly clean a house like that every day for the gift of sight."

This story not only made me look at Nina with increased appreciation, but it also challenged me. It's so much easier to write and speak than to do the ministry of "grubby tasks," but when it's all over, Jesus is going to value the hands-on, caring ministries above all others (see Matt. 25:31-46). We need to keep that in mind.

If I speak in the tongues of men and of angels, but have not love, I am only a resounding gong or a clanging cymbal (1 Cor. 13:1).

No Other Way

Nearly 45 years ago, when I was almost 20, I gave my heart to the Lord. It was a most unlikely event, for up until that time I had considered religion a necessary discipline for my elders, but certainly not for me. Though I endured some of the trappings for conscience' sake, I secretly envisioned the future as a long bright journey, free of all holy restraints. With my healthy young body and my eager creative mind, I'd swing on every rainbow and eat stardust for breakfast.

Then, ironically, I became the owner of a set of rather somber-looking books—religious books, no less. Even their collective title was a bit overwhelming—The Conflict of the Ages. Not exactly exciting fare for a frivolous 19-year-old, but I was a reader and not just a frivolous one, either. I did indeed plow through a lot of novels at that period, but I still enjoyed a good biography, and actually read the *National Geographic* instead of just looking at the pictures. So I wasn't too intimidated by the awesome set of books, which started out with Lucifer's rebellion in heaven and ended with the second coming of Christ.

I opened the first one, intending only to browse—and ended up reading all five volumes cover to cover. It took a long while, but it was the most fascinating reading I'd ever done, and the most life-changing. When I finished, I no longer saw life as something through which I would stride, maneuvering and manipulating, while filling my apron with the ripest plums.

I saw myself as a sinner, as a small speck in a great universe for whom Jesus Himself had to die. It stripped away all my illusions, yet left me with a fresh excitement and a sweet hope that has remained until this very day.

In my new love for the Carpenter-God I made positive changes in my life and attitudes—righted wrongs and confessed sins. I wanted Him to know that I was on His team, that I was grateful for His inconceivable rescue. It was all joy. And it has lasted, wavering sometimes in intensity, but always there.

In the past few years, however, I've noted a change. Some of the joy has felt more like apprehension. And my Carpenter Friend has been showing me some rather ugly things about myself.

I had been vaguely aware of them all along, but suddenly He said, "We've been together all these years, and those flaws are still there.

Why are you hugging them so tightly?"

"I'm not," I replied defensively. "I can drop them anytime. No problem."

But I couldn't. I'd tried, and even had brief successes, but no lasting victories.

I reminded God of His promise in Hebrews 10:16—"I will put my laws in their hearts, and I will write them on their minds."

"I always thought this process of growth was automatic," I said, "as long as I stayed committed to You. I really want freedom from these sins. Why are You not helping me?"

"I am," He answered gently, "but you always draw back when it becomes painful."

Painful! I'd thought sanctification was natural and comfortable, something hardly to be noticed. I could click off quite a few things I'd left behind without undue discomfort. What was He talking about?

"We're down now to your cherished sins," He said, still tender. "The real work is just beginning. You must suffer. There is no other way. But I'll be with you."

Suddenly, as though endowed with 20/20 spiritual vision, I realized all the ways in which He'd been presenting opportunities for me to grow, and all the ways in which I'd been rejecting them. Because—yes, He was right—because I hated the demands they made upon me. Could I learn to live in a state of discomfort, for Him, until His ways became mine? When self dies, it hurts. Could I deal with that? Not alone, for sure. "You'll stay with me?" I asked, scared.

"Always," He promised, and I heard the smile in His voice.

So that's where we're at right now, my Carpenter Friend and I. Sometimes I still run, but I'm trying to learn about the pain of becoming a new person, because He knows all about pain, and I want to share even that with Him.

Rejoice that you participate in the sufferings of Christ, so that you may be overjoyed when his glory is revealed (1 Peter 4:13).

Homecoming

Morning is breaking, and I'm watching it as we climb toward 32,000 feet. Watching North Dakota unroll between wispy little puffs of white. Finally there's nothing beneath but a great sea of white cotton candy. Sometimes in that sea there are misty grottoes and huge curling breakers where heavenly surfers must surely come to romp and test their skills.

I am going home. Those must be the sweetest words in any language. Going home. I am a home person. With all apologies to Betty Friedan, I like cooking and cleaning, puttering in the garden, and having our married kids roll in on Saturday night with their families. That's my idea of the perfect life. But God had other plans for me—at least part-time—for this fearful child of His who never liked to fly, never liked to leave home, and who got lost in airports. Gently He led me along.

At first I took no speaking engagements unless Don was able to go with me. Then came the entry of women's retreats. One does not take her husband to a women's retreat. So put your hand in God's and go alone, June. Do it until boarding an airplane is like boarding a bus and until airports are only places where one follows the signs. Do it until fear backs off, though for me it always remains in a corner leering and waiting to pounce.

Tonight is Eric's second birthday. I want to be home for his celebration. I want to see him laugh when the locomotive I bought him puffs real smoke. I want to hear what happened to everyone at home this weekend while I've been gone. And I want to tell them about the retreat. I want to share with them the stories Anne Wham told me as we rode to the airport in darkness this morning.

Anne is just back from helping with an evangelistic crusade in the Ukraine, and her tender heart is still bruised from the deprivation she witnessed. As she described the chaotic lifestyle there, more and more I appreciated home. We talked of America, this beautiful land that has been so richly blessed, and we admitted sadly that our government is corrupt, our economy staggering, but it is still home, where there are groceries on the shelves and cars in our garages. (This may not be our situation for long, but in this moment there is yet golden America for many.)

She told me of money that was being raised to fling out the gospel seed while the ground lies fallow. I would like to be part of that, wouldn't you? Because I want all God's people who've endured years of persecution, famine, poverty, to go home, really home. Not just home to microwaves and good health-care plans, but home to be with Jesus, where whatever our needs shall be, they will be met.

Beyond lush fruit and garments of shining white, I long for spiritual wholeness, long to lay aside the constant conflict with self, long to look—in perfect peace—into the eyes of Him whom I've followed in faith, and know that, at last, I am truly done journeying.

Let us stay out of the malls, friends, and feed the hungry, both spiritually and physically. Let's get the work done.

When Anne's daughter was offered a shopping trip to purchase new clothes for college, she said, "No thanks, Mom. After being in the Ukraine, I don't need new clothes for college." Bravo! May we all line up behind her.

No longer will they build houses and others live in them, or plant and others eat. For as the days of a tree, so will be the days of my people; my chosen ones will long enjoy the works of their hands (Isa. 65:22).

Operation Rescue

Going to the backyard to hang some laundry, I noticed our fluffy black cat sitting under the maple at the back door. He's a handsome fellow with round yellow eyes who usually tumbles into an affectionate heap at the sight of any human, hoping for a tummy rub.

But this day there was something in his stance that told me he had temporarily reverted to his sinister feline heritage. This was a side of him of which I was not fond, and I looked about for his victim. Sure enough, there among last year's dead leaves a tiny chipmunk hopped hopefully in the direction of a tree, a little dazed but still intact.

Being well versed in cat strategies, I knew Spook would allow the chipmunk only a few moments of freedom before he pounced upon it once more. These cruel games so distress me that I decided to intervene.

Waving my hands and shouting, I was able to distract the cat long enough for the chipmunk to make it to the tree. Spook hissed at me angrily, made a flying leap toward the tree, and actually picked the fleeing chipmunk right off the trunk about three feet from the ground. I had to admit it was a magnificent maneuver, but I still had no intentions of abandoning the rescue operation.

Once more, making a loud racket, I chased him, flapping a wet towel. Unused to such antics on my part, he dropped his prey and raced around the corner of the house. I stayed about awhile to be sure that he didn't return and that the chipmunk made a safe exit.

When it was all over and I was hanging clothes on the line, I realized how silly it had all been. Spook is an eager and skilled hunter who has his fill of rodents daily. He, in fact, often leaves his excess upon the back step as though wishing to share his booty with us. We have valued his expertise as an exterminator.

So why had I made such a production over one chipmunk? Because slow death is ugly, and chipmunks are adorable (though destructive). Because I hate knowing a gentle loved pet is capable of cruel torture. Because the whole system seems so wrong.

Then my thoughts took another turn. I had been deeply concerned for the chipmunk and totally angry with the cat. I could not, conscientiously, have left the scene until the chipmunk's safety was ensured. A life-and-death battle was going on, and I had a moral responsibility to step between the victim and the villain.

The Bible warns that the devil is going about as a roaring lion (another fearful feline), seeking whom he may devour. Have I ever been as concerned about his victims as about the chipmunk?

Do I feel a righteous anger at his subtle, cruel strategies?

All about me my fellow humans succumb to his wiles, suffer in his clutches, think they are free when he's only waiting to pounce once again.

And I go about my business, seeing, knowing, convincing myself that it's no concern of mine, as though a chipmunk were of more value than a child of God.

Of course, if the devil could be routed with the flicking of a wet towel, we'd have been rid of him long ago, but unfortunately, he possesses powers far beyond ours, and our only safety lies in submitting ourselves to Christ, who, praise God, is a strong and sure defense.

But what of those who are ignorant of or indifferent to His care? Am I diligent in my efforts to introduce them to the divine strategy for rescue, or is it easier to look neither left nor right, figuring we're all on our own?

These are the questions I asked myself the day I rescued a chipmunk.

Your enemy the devil prowls around like a roaring lion looking for someone to devour (1 Peter 5:8).

Like a Thief in the Night

Amy, our youngest, was making the 400-mile trip home from college with friends. They would drop her off at our exit along the expressway in the wee hours, around 1:00 or 2:00 a.m. Over the phone we discussed the mechanics of this operation and decided that a practical solution would be to leave one of our cars parked at the exit's commuter lot so she could simply hop in and drive home.

"We'll wake up and greet you when you arrive," I assured her.

"That's foolish," she chided. "The whole point of leaving the car at the exit is so you don't have to get up in the middle of the night."

"Well, we're looking forward to a few moments of chatting, no matter what the hour."

"You're being ridiculous, Mom. We'll have 10 days to chat before I have to go back. Get your rest."

I didn't pursue the matter further, but when we retired that night, sometime after 11:00, I said to my husband, "She'll probably be home in less than three hours. It's going to be so great to see her. I don't mind being awakened at all."

It was all clear in my mind. The dog would bark from his rug in the back hall. The ascending garage door would rattle noisily in response to the automatic opener. As Amy passed our door on the way to her own room I'd call out, "Welcome home," and she'd come in and sit on the bed and tell us about her trip. Maybe she'd even be hungry, and I'd get up and fix her a snack. In this climate of anticipation I fell asleep.

Sometime later I awoke, victim of the foggy confusion born of deep sleep. Something was special about this night. What was it? Oh, yes, Amy was coming home. I raised up on one elbow to see the clock better, squinting fiercely to bring the red numerals into focus. Six minutes after 4:00. A wave of terror swept over me. Where was she? I never had liked the idea of leaving the car at the exit. What tragedy had befallen her?

Suddenly I realized the room was very dark. When we had gone to bed we'd left all the outside lights on to welcome her home. They'd lit up our bedroom like a streetlamp. Those lights were very definitely out. What did that mean?

Well, dummy, I said to myself after forcing my sleep-numbed brain into gear, *it means she's home.* Somehow she'd arrived, turned out the lights, and gone to bed without waking man or beast. I'd have to face her teasing in the morning.

I couldn't go back to sleep. That moment of fear had pumped too much adrenaline into my system. My thoughts were disconnected. The dog must be getting old, or maybe he was just too smart to bark at someone who'd been his best friend for 10 years. Maybe it was we who were getting old. Or maybe Don's first double round of golf for the season and my hours of heavy-duty housecleaning had simply been good sleeping pills.

I thought of my preconceived picture of Amy's arrival, which hadn't worked out according to plan at all. (Next morning I learned she'd parked at the driveway entrance and tiptoed to her room, being careful of creaky floorboards and noisy door latches.)

A Bible verse kept nibbling at my mind. "Watch ye therefore: for ye know not when the master of the house cometh, at even, or at midnight, or at the cockcrowing, or in the morning: lest coming suddenly he find you sleeping" (Mark 13:35, 36, KJV).

I had a neat picture in my mind of that arrival, too. Was it possible my smug scenario for that event might not be totally accurate either? That I could be caught unawares?

Thankful for the quiet darkness, I prayed, *O Lord, let me be ready. Busy about Your work. Filled with Your Spirit. Watchful. Alert. Never too sure, too confident. Never sleeping. May my spiritual alarm clock always be set. Let the lights of my welcome be polished and shining, my eyes lifted up, and my arms open wide. "Even so, come, Lord Jesus" [Rev. 22:20, KJV].*

So you also must be ready, because the Son of Man will come at an hour when you do not expect him (Matt. 24:44).

Sacred Sevens

We are expecting our seventh grandchild in a few weeks. The next youngest is going on 2, and we've all been enjoying his toddlerhood so much that we haven't discussed the newcomer as extensively as one does sometimes when siblings are spaced further apart. But as his mother grows larger and speaks of the vigorous movements of the child within, I begin to grow excited. What a mystery an unborn child is! No sonogram this time. Boy or girl?

His—or her—mother doesn't really care. She's enjoyed her first small son so much that another would suit her just fine . . . but then, there are all those ruffly little dresses in the department stores.

Obviously, we'll all praise God for whatever gender arrives. A new little person is a great gift to any family.

I find the idea fascinating that he/she will be seventh in line. I like the number 7 because God likes it and surely attaches some significance to it. Revelation is full of sevens—seven churches, seven golden lampstands, seven stars, seven seals, seven angels, seven trumpets, seven plagues, seven bowls. Did I get them all?

And then, of course, there's the most meaningful seven of all, the seventh day. Sometimes I wonder if God sprinkled sevens throughout Revelation as little flags of encouragement to all who have honored the Sabbath of Genesis 2:2, 3. As though before His Holy Book was closed, He gave a last affirmation to the faithfulness of those who'd remained loyal to His holy day, and those who would continue to guard its sacredness even to the death.

We are so accustomed to our Sabbath routine that sometimes I fear we lose sight of the wonder of a 24-hour period in which to socialize with God. Sometimes it just ends up in socializing with our friends. Occasionally we get so deep into entertaining, good deeds, napping, that we have not a moment for the magic God planned. Often on the second Sabbath of camp meeting we simply stay home. We sit in the prayer garden and read, just Don and I, then discuss what we are learning. We might take a walk, and sometime during the day have a private and precious time of prayer. When the sun slips into the west, invariably I feel it's been the sweetest day of the year. I vow that somehow I'll incorporate its peace into every Sabbath.

There's such a satisfaction in spending a long, uninterrupted expanse of time with God. I know corporate worship is essential. I enjoy it. And surely we need to share the Sabbath blessing with those ill or burdened, but perhaps once a month we could simply nurture our friendship with Jesus in the afternoon. No guests, no activities—just a sweet time alone with the Lord. That seventh portion of the week isn't half long enough. I've come to treasure every aspect of it.

So when our little mystery baby comes along behind Christopher, Jenny, Lisa, Vincent, Nicky, and Eric, I'm going to watch carefully to see if this is a special child. For sure he'll (she'll?) be a special child to us, even though one's place in the lineup probably doesn't have significance. And that babe will be special to God, just as every child is, just as you and I are. We may not be seventh in any genealogy, but we are children of the King, and doesn't that challenge you to live up to your royal role?

If you call the Sabbath a delight and the Lord's holy day honorable, and if you honor it by not going your own way and not doing as you

please or speaking idle words, then you will find your joy in the Lord, and I will cause you to ride on the heights of the land (Isa. 58:13, 14).

Thoughts on Losing a Son

September had robbed me, and now she was trying to make amends with red vines on stone walls. Such charms, I must admit, did compensate to some small degree for my loss, but it was with a heavy heart that I tramped her stubbled fields.

We had driven our oldest son to Union Springs, New York, for his first year at boarding academy. With joy we had purchased new clothes, rugs, bedspread, blankets, sheets, towels, wastebasket, drapes—even a pencil sharpener.

With him we weathered the registration lines, the schedule-planning lines, and the work assignment sector. Together we settled his room, and, as I made up his bed with brand-new sheets, some brand-new emotions began to inflict themselves, all uninvited, upon me.

Out in the hall I heard very casual farewells going on. I must swallow this lump in my throat and get on with the bed making. I'm always too emotional. We stored small items in drawers, large ones in cupboards, hung familiar clothes in an unfamiliar closet. We puttered and made small talk until there was nothing left with which to putter.

At which point our six-foot son, with his spanking-fresh driver's license, said very offhandedly, "You'll have to keep an eye on the gas gauge, Mom. I won't be there to fill it up for you."

And I said, "You know I'll never remember." That was our farewell. (Now I understood the casual goodbyes in the hall.) My heart stomped its feet and screamed, "I cannot take this," but my lips smiled and said inconsequentials.

Boots with a metal tap on the heel that always told me when he was around, faded jeans with a tiny mend on the back pocket, white even teeth in a smile that had warmed our hearts for 16 years. I would tuck the picture away in my mind, for he'd never be quite the same again. In the independence of dormitory life youth achieves a self-sufficiency that snaps the apron string abruptly. When we met again, self-confidence would have replaced the wistfulness in his eyes.

On the way home we treated the younger children to milk shakes, filled our trunk with apples and peaches from one of the many fruit stands along the way, and everything was normal, except my heart that ached, and my ears that kept listening for the missing voice, the absent laughter. I wondered, riding along, how God said goodbye to His only Son. (I had others.) Did They touch each other in farewell, or did They fear, as did I, that the moment was too fragile?

One of my favorite writers penned these words: "It was a struggle, even with the King of the universe, to yield up His Son" (*Patriarchs and Prophets*, p. 63). If so, did He too bow broken and sorrowing as He watched the manger drama unfold on Planet Earth, knowing it had to be, wanting it to be, but unable to silence His father-heart?

In the wonderful book *The Desire of Ages* there are two paragraphs that suddenly mean a great deal more to me. Let me share them with you. "Satan in heaven had hated Christ for His position in the courts of God. He hated Him the more when he himself was dethroned. He hated Him who pledged Himself to redeem a race of sinners. Yet into the world where Satan claimed dominion God permitted His Son to come, a helpless babe, subject to the weakness of humanity. He permitted Him to meet life's peril in common with every human soul, to fight the battle as every child of humanity must fight it, at the risk of failure and eternal loss.

"The heart of the human father yearns over his son. He looks into the face of his little child, and trembles at the thought of life's peril. He longs to shield his dear one from Satan's power, to hold him back from temptation and conflict. To meet a bitterer conflict and a more fearful risk, God gave His only-begotten Son, that the path of life might be made sure for our little ones. 'Herein is love.' Wonder, O heavens! and be astonished, O earth!" (p. 49).

Thanks be to God for his indescribable gift! (2 Cor. 9:15).

He That Taketh Not His Cross
. . . Is Not Worthy

Surrounded with roses, bird song, and the splashing of water in the fountain, I sat in my prayer garden in the early morning. I had come to this spot, as was my custom, to spend a few minutes with God. There were no roses and bird song within my heart, however—only frustration and despair. Our family was all out of kilter, many of its members struggling with what seemed insurmountable problems. No matter how fast I ran, I couldn't meet their needs. To make matters worse, I had some rusty old sins of my own. I felt a failure as a parent, as a wife, and as a Christian.

My lovely garden mocked me. What was I doing in it? I had tended this spot with elaborate care, had in fact given up all my other gardens that this one might exhibit weed-free perfection. I had dedicated it to the worship of God and always entered it reverently. Even the hours I spent weeding here were blessed. Usually. Today I wondered. Was there any virtue in a weed-free garden if the gardener's heart resembled a bramble patch?

I didn't bother to outline my disappointments to God this morning (nor am I going to to you, my friend, for they are too personal). I had spread them out before Him so many times that I began to wonder if He too were sick of hearing about them. I just sat there, an ugly blight on the bright morning.

My eyes rested on a thriving clump of coralbells. Coralbells happen to be one of my favorite flowers, but this clump was special for other reasons. A writer friend had left it on my doorstep one May morning a few years before with a note that said "From my ordinary garden to your prayer garden. Love, Kay." I'd planted it with delight, and each spring delicate stems of coralbells rose from the healthy patch of deep-green leaves to remind me of a valued friendship. Now thoughts of Kay penetrated my own depression. I'd had a note from her not so long before in which she'd explained her absence from gatherings of our mutual friends. She'd written, "I'm going through a troublesome time. My heart is so heavy I cannot create. I cannot think. I'm barely existing."

Well, Kay, I said to myself, *that makes two of us.*

I wondered how she was coping. She had always impressed me as such a strong, steady person. Come to think of it, that's how people have always seen me, too. Here's a bulletin for the world: Even strong, steady people hurt sometimes. Hurt desperately. Usually they can't unburden themselves to others, can't put their heads down on shoulders for a good cry, can't believe anyone would be willing to listen.

Putting aside my thoughts of Kay, I turned to the Gospel of Matthew in the Bible. My eyes fell on a short, familiar text. I read it over several times: "Anyone who does not take his cross and follow me is not worthy of me" (Matt. 10:38).

I had always wondered just what it meant to take up a cross. What was the cross? Some tragedy, like going blind? Some act of sacrifice, like going as a missionary to a remote corner of earth? Some denial, such as living a Spartan life when one had the means for luxury?

There in the sunshine, with my leaden heart, it occurred to me that perhaps each person's cross is simply the difficulties of his or her own life—the "troublesome time," as Kay had put it. It also occurred to me that if I took up the cross (I expect that means I must stop fighting against it) and followed Christ, I would have to trust His leading. After all, one doesn't follow a leader in whom he or she lacks confidence. I had been following Christ for 30 years.

Most of the time His yoke had been reasonably easy, His burden light. But now He was saying, "Put a cross on your back, June. That's really what following Me is all about. You've been in training a long time." Somehow the coralbells and the cross were all intermingled in my mind. The coralbells represented love—the cross, discipline. Or did it? Maybe the cross represented love too.

That cross which hung Him like a bloody banner over the earth must have been a cross of love—His love for you and me. And come to think of it, the cross He had handed me was going to take a lot of love too, if I took it up and carried it. I wondered if I had enough love. Maybe if I placed my feet day by day in His footsteps, He'd provide the love as we went along.

I picked a stalk of coralbells to send to Kay. Maybe we could carry our crosses side by side, behind Him. I'd talk to her about it.

I want to know Christ . . . and the fellowship of sharing in his sufferings (Phil. 3:10).

A Sermon on the Runway

We sat on the crowded plane awaiting takeoff—my husband, our youngest daughter, and I. Already my head was splitting. I am not an air traveler. I am ever conscious of my country roots when hustling around airports. All the confused sophistication is not for me. I am never more aware of my mortality than when lifted into the sky on that thrust of power and steel. Only necessity or convenience sends me up into that space beyond the clouds.

This day necessity had ruled, and I resigned myself to a long cross-country flight. Beyond the tiny windows, rain began to fall, splattering into dark-gray spots on the summer-dry concrete. I was grateful for the instruments in the cockpit that would enable the pilot to guide us safely through the murk. (It so happened that we ricocheted about in an electrical storm for 15 or 20 minutes after takeoff, but I was blissfully unaware of that future development at the moment.)

As the rain beat more furiously upon the pavement and my headache worsened (husband and daughter chatting contentedly at my side, comfortably immune to my discomfort and apprehension), I noted a tiny patch of grass that had forced its way through a crack in the runway. It had reached maturity, and its small seed heads blew softly in the wind. I could almost feel its thirsty pleasure in the rain. A miniature prairie in a world of concrete. Something about that patch of grass reaching up to the summer rain soothed the tensions tightening within me. I reveled in all the sensations of pleasure the earth has always afforded. The band of pain encircling my head eased. A dozen or so blades of grass had changed the tenor of my thoughts.

Days later, when my work was completed, we saw the rolling hills of eastern Washington, green with new wheat. We saw the snowfields of Mount Rainier pink in the light of early evening. Once, at sunset, we stopped along the highway to photograph a flat golden field, dotted with black cattle and backdropped with hazy, blue hills. We saw the Golden Gate Bridge suspended in fog, and walked among wild lupine in the mountains of southern California.

But that little patch of grass at the Toronto airport said more to me than all the splendors that followed. Under the most adverse circumstances it had fulfilled its mission, somehow managing to look lovely in the process. And to this weary traveler it had whispered a message in the rain: *Calm down. God is everywhere, even in this fast-paced world. In the places where rain falls in hidden valleys and violets flower where no one comes* to see. *But if His peace is in your heart, it will go with you through the skies and into urban centers where all is madness. He is not limited to Edens. You must bring His rest to the frantic places. That's your mission.*

Could it be that I who so withdraw from freeways and skyscrapers, from airports and subways, from crowded streets and neon lights, could possibly carry His peace with me into those places? That I could be rain and wind and summer grasses to a scurrying world?

Not just me, but His followers everywhere. That's the assignment. Reflecting Him in the most impossible places. Being a new creature in the most unlikely circumstances. Scattering love where love has died. Singing when there's no music. Laughing because God is king, and nothing can touch that, or change it, or diminish it.

As the plane turned and roared, at last, down the runway, I said softly in farewell, " 'Who shall separate us from the love of Christ?' Not crowds, or buses, or confusion. Not highways, or hotels, or ghettos. Not loneliness, or poverty, or hate. 'In all these things we are more than conquerors through Him who loved us.' " (Apologies to the apostle Paul.)

Be joyful always; pray continually; give thanks in all circumstances, for this is God's will for you in Christ Jesus (1 Thess. 5:16-18).

Enemy in the Garden

There is a snake in my garden. He's close to three feet long and about the circumference of a garden hose. I hope it's a he, because one is plenty. My husband counsels me to leave him alone because he helps keep the pest count down. Frankly, I do not like him, not in my garden or anywhere else. Fortunately he stays in a particular area, and I have not yet come upon him in an unexpected spot. Our guess is that he lives under a large low rock around which he is often sunning. When on his turf, I am usually careful to make plenty of noise and shake the plants about with a garden tool before working among them.

Today on my way back to the house from an hour's work in the late afternoon sun, I stopped, momentarily, to pull a few weeds from a clump of blue fescue. As I thrust my hand deep into the spiky grass, it

141

began to open a path of its own, a weaving noiseless path. I let out a yelp as I caught sight of the long slithering body gliding by my hand. I should have respected his territory and given him an evacuation notice, but when I don't see him for several days I forget about him or tell myself he's moved on. In theory, having him there doesn't seem too horrendous, but when I'm actually watching him execute his undulating exit, I want him out of my garden, gone from my presence permanently. He is horrible. My apologies to snake-lovers, but he is horrible.

There are many kinds of loathsome critters . . . spiders, rats, cockroaches, and bedbugs (to name a few), but there's something different about a snake. Something evil. It's just not normal to have no legs. Even mosquitoes have legs! That terrible, silent slithering does not belong on this planet. I guess I could tolerate him better if he squeaked or chirped or even growled.

I wonder, as I watch this repulsive creature, how he relates to Genesis 3:14—"You will crawl on your belly and you will eat dust all the days of your life." The Bible does not do much to satisfy our curiosity, saying only that "the serpent was more crafty than any of the wild animals" (verse 1). As we place the story of Eve's temptation alongside the rest of the Bible, we must conclude that Satan used the serpent as a vehicle for his own devious ends. That triggers some questions for me. Why, then, did it matter whether or not the serpent was crafty? Why was the serpent punished if it was only the mouthpiece?

These aren't vital questions, nor essential to our salvation. But seeing a snake does always remind me of the sad drama in Eden. Maybe God planned it that way.

Probably the important lesson the snake can teach us is that God cannot tolerate sin. Much as He loved Adam and Eve, much as He enjoyed His brand-new creation and longed to see it progress as planned, He (with an aching heart, I'm sure) had to call it all to a halt. To deal with sin head-on. It hurt Him as well as us. Plan B involved infinite suffering for both Father and Son. Sin is ugly, like the snake. We pilgrims from this planet who enter heaven will be wide-eyed with wonder. We have no conception of a sinless environment. What will it be like to live without the forces of evil tugging us downward?

I'm looking forward to strolling with Eve in her garden and learning from her new skills and techniques. What a long nightmare it's been between her serpent and my snake, but, praise God, our gardens there will be free of both and all they represent! Come, Lord Jesus.

But in keeping with his promise we are looking forward to a new heaven and a new earth, the home of righteousness (2 Peter 3:13).

A Collage of Weddings

Sometimes on rainy summer days when I was growing up in the home of my paternal grandparents, boredom drove me to their bedroom closet. There, after forcing my way through rows of hanging garments, in a dim nook under the eaves, I opened a small trunk containing the few remaining mementos of my mother, who had died following my birth. A half-sewn baby garment with the rusting needle piercing the cloth, just as she had left it; a packet of good poetry (her own creations, tied with blue ribbon); a wall mirror on which she'd painted a trailing spray of flowers around one corner. The remnants of her 19 years. There was one more thing in the tiny trunk—her wedding dress. No glistening satin extravaganza for this Depression-era Vermont girl. Something semi-practical that could be worn again on grand occasions. It was a "flapper" dress, very short, soft coral in color, a large fabric flower at the line where the long-waisted top met the flouncy bottom. The kind of dress girls did the Charleston in.

My aunt told me that Mother was tall and angular, but surprisingly graceful in all her movements. She liked to hunt with my father, and I imagined her moving through the forest noiselessly as an Indian.

But enough of that! I really want to talk, at this season of the year, about wedding dresses—my mother's, my own, my daughter's.

I borrowed my wedding gown, wanting the satin extravaganza even though I could not afford it. My cousin, born to a more affluent heritage and matching my tall, scrawny figure well enough, generously lent me hers. Never mind that the train stretched halfway down the aisle of the tiny church. In my borrowed finery, given away by a friend of the groom's parents whom I hardly knew, I entered the marital state. Nevertheless, the vows held, and 43 years later I can chuckle about it, at least about the dress, if not about my voluntarily absent father.

Everything was right for our daughter's wedding. Our credit card was at her disposal, and she chose a lovely, though not extravagant, gown. She tried on an exquisitely beaded headpiece, but laid it aside as too expensive. "This is once in a lifetime," I insisted, placing it alongside the chosen gown, deaf to her practical horror.

Her father bore her proudly, and a little sadly, down the aisle. I wished my mother might have been there in her coral dress to sit beside me and share the magic moment.

But there is a wedding garment far more important than my

mother's '20s creation or our daughter's white satin. John the revelator says:

> "For the wedding of the Lamb has come
> and his bride has made herself ready.
> Fine linen, bright and clean, was *given* her to wear"
> (Rev. 19:7, 8).

The traditional interpretation of these verses would undoubtedly identify the bride as Christ's church, but in that context it could surely also represent each of us as individual members of the church body.

It's interesting to note that the garment is a gift. No need to borrow or go into debt. It's also noteworthy that the bride has expended the effort to put on the gown and "make herself ready."

What is this garment that has been provided for our wedding to the Lamb? Though John's prophetic writings were often veiled in mystery, in this case he answers our question quickly and clearly. "Fine linen stands for the righteous acts of the saints" (verse 8).

Isaiah, long years before, spoke of this gift of clothing in much the same way: "I delight greatly in the Lord; my soul rejoices in my God. For he has clothed me with garments of salvation and arrayed me in a robe of righteousness, . . . as a bride adorns herself with her jewels" (Isa. 61:10).

And so in faith I put on the lovely garment of righteousness, knowing I do not merit it, but that I cannot take part in the marriage ceremony without it. I must not make the mistake of attempting to fabricate a garment for myself. The Bible is clear that all my righteousness is as filthy rags. No fine linen whatsoever (Isa. 64:6).

I am so grateful that my Bridegroom is the creator of righteous acts and shining garments and that, unlike my father, He will arrive with great joy and celebration at the wedding. This bride intends to sparkle in His gift of fine linen, bright and clean.

He who overcomes will . . . be dressed in white (Rev. 3:5).

Camp Meeting Encounter

She came to me at camp meeting. I was the morning speaker, and she was an old woman, bent with age but strong in spirit. I sensed she'd never bothered much with senior citizens' benefits nor acknowledged the passing years. Life was for living. She was a no-nonsense kind of woman.

She told me in a thin, plaintive voice of the four children she'd brought to camp meeting and the minor problem she was having with one of them.

"Four children!" I gasped. "What are you doing with four children?"

"They're not mine," she said, trying to be patient with this none-too-bright camp meeting speaker. "They belong to a friend. I take care of them some. I asked their mother, 'Could they come to camp meeting?' She said, 'Sure.' "

"Are you in an RV?" I asked, trying to visualize this frail little person riding herd on her borrowed family at an age when most kept busy just surviving.

"I'm in a tent," she advised tartly, as though that's where any self-respecting camper belonged.

Later I discovered her canvas domain pitched among those bordering the walkway to the main auditorium. I passed it every morning on my way to my speaking appointment. I noticed her pouring bowls of Cheerios breakfast cereal and prodding sleepy little ones into clothing. She chided them gently in her querulous old voice, but I read the fondness in their eyes.

One morning as I passed, she motioned me to stop, and I welcomed the opportunity to chat. I was developing a tremendous respect for this individual who'd surely passed threescore and 10, yet didn't count herself too old for the stresses of child care.

She mentioned a concern she bore and wanted me to address from the pulpit. I declined, but said playfully to a lovely dark-eyed little girl at her side, "Who is this lady, anyway?"

The little one leaned her head against her benefactor's arm and said, with infinite love, "She's my 'Noodle.' " Somehow the ridiculous nickname should have been disrespectful, but it was, instead, funny and endearing, embroidered with hearts and flowers.

The dear saint looked a bit embarrassed at the child's use of the familiar appellation. "They call me that 'cause it sounds like my last name," she explained brusquely. " 'Twas all they could manage when they were small, and it stuck."

I walked away knowing I'd never forget the busy little tent, the harried woman with fine white wisps curling about her face, and the adoring child clinging to her arm. Some of us are so eloquent, so glib with our Christian patter. Some of us are doctrinal giants, furiously debating the fine points of the law. Some live meticulous lives, determined to gain eternity by the avoidance of a single sin. Some dutifully minister when it can hardly be avoided. But "Noodle" volunteered. I doubt she concerned herself overmuch with theology, but she knew the worth of a little child. She did not excuse herself as too old or too frail. She counted the rigors of camp meeting as nothing, that her small charges might learn more of Jesus. Her simple witness challenged and accused me. What did I know of such humble, unsung ministry?

When the Master welcomes her home, surely He will hug her, smile, and whisper, "Thank you, Noodle; thank you for tending My lambs."

Jesus said, "Feed my lambs" (John 21:15).

The Brother Who Went on Before

One day I was reading the judgment scene in Daniel 7. It always fascinates me, as it must have fascinated Daniel. Actually, the Bible says it disturbed and troubled him (verse 15), this court drama unfolding before his eyes. He had no way to fit the scene into a time frame. You and I well understand the centuries that rumbled on before the vision became reality. Past the Messiah, past the early church, past the Reformation. But Daniel, locked in his own era, saw only a great mystery.

Like a breathtaking TV special:

thrones set in place
the Ancient of Days enters
clothing white as snow
hair white like wool.
His throne flames with fire,

its wheels ablaze.
A river of fire coming out before Him.
Are you trying to wrap your mind about this "science fiction"?
Thousands upon thousands attend
this majestic King of the universe
Ten thousand times ten thousand
stand before Him.
The court comes to order
and books are opened.
What is written in those books?
Surely Daniel holds his breath—what is about to take place?

It's the next scene that moved me to tears the first time its meaning really hit me.

Daniel continues: "I looked, and there before me was one like a son of man" (verse 13).

In other words, into this great pageant of heavenly beings, angels by the millions and other creatures upon which Daniel had never laid eyes before, came a human being. Completely out of his realm. Remember, Daniel had not seen Jesus walking about Galilee, or hanging upon a cross. All he had was a dusty dream of a Messiah to come. So when he saw this citizen of Planet Earth walking among the great shining residents of heaven, I expect he did what you and I would call, in twentieth century parlance, a double take. And then, wonder of wonders, this Earth-Man walked right into the presence of the Ancient of Days, and as if that were not enough, the Earth-Man received authority, glory, and power.

I could well visualize Daniel's astonishment, but beyond that for the first time, reality hit me. Jesus is really up there in His human skin, one of us. Now and forever. Whenever the salvation process becomes remote and begins to dim for me, I go back to this chapter and sit with Daniel and watch the scene unfold. I long to take the prophet by the arm and shout, "That's *Him*, Daniel. That's the Messiah. The very Son of God, so much one of us that you couldn't pick Him out on a city street."

The following quotation has become very dear to me, for it seems but an extension of the Daniel 7 portrait of Jesus.

"In Christ we become more closely united to God than if we had never fallen. In taking our nature, the Saviour has bound Himself to humanity by a tie that is never to be broken. Through the eternal ages He is linked with us. . . . He gave Him not only to bear our sins, and to die as our sacrifice; *He gave Him to the fallen race.* . . . God gave His only-begotten Son to become one of the human family, *forever to retain His human nature*" (*The Desire of Ages*, p. 25; italics supplied).

It's enough to send us to our knees in joyous, humble gratitude throughout eternity.

For God so loved the world, that he gave his only begotten Son, that whosoever believeth in him should not perish, but have everlasting life (John 3:16, KJV).

Conversation in the Chapel

There was something God wanted me to do, and I didn't want to do it. Not at all.

I had been wrestling with the problem all day, endeavoring to convince myself it wasn't necessary that I minister to this individual in need. I wasn't sure how to go about it, or even if it was possible. Once I became involved in the situation, however, there was no telling what demands it might make upon me and my tidy life. I was a jumble of fear, guilt, selfishness, and dread.

That evening I attended a candlelight Communion service. Winter winds hurled blinding snow across icy roads outside, but within our cozy chapel all was warmth and beauty. Candles flickered against stained glass, flowers glowed softly in the semidarkness, and I was surrounded by my church family. People whose values were my values. Who lived their lives in disciplined, dependable ways. At my side sat a dear and loved friend with whom I could pray and counsel.

"Lord," I said, "this is my world. Everything is orderly. The testimonies tonight have all been eloquent witnesses to Your presence working in committed lives.

"You know how I love beauty and order, Lord. And You also know how this intrusion into our home would create confusion and disarray. You understand how my writing schedule would suffer. And what about the deadline that hovers threateningly over my head? You can't really be asking this of me, can You?"

And there in the softly lighted chapel, He said, "June, I too love order and beauty. That's how heaven is. Not a leaf out of place, everything breathtaking in its exquisite perfection. If you think these candles and poinsettias are lovely, you will be absolutely staggered by the visual stimuli of heaven.

"And there's a serenity here beyond your earthly imaginings. All the tensions with which you are familiar are wondrously absent. No envy, no deceit, no jealousy. No angry outbursts or sullen silences. Just a spirit of love, rather like what you are experiencing here in the chapel, only magnified a million times.

"We have testimony times here, too. Only instead of sharing the pains and problems of life, the residents center their attention upon praise. They couldn't think of a pain or problem if they pondered an eon or two.

"And you mentioned friends. Well, there is a touching loyalty among the dwellers here for Me and My Father. Their love reaches out almost tangibly as I walk among them. It's very peaceful and comfortable here, dear one.

"A long time ago, however, My Father asked something of Me, too. It wasn't easy what He asked of Me. It took Me away from Him, from this fair land, and from the adoration of angels. It threw Me into an alien environment in which the people didn't know much about My kind of life. Nor did they want to. For 33 years I lived in an atmosphere of rejection. Even the landscaping was pretty flawed. But I had a mission to fulfill because He had asked something of Me, My Father. So I slept on the ground beneath the stars, suffered insults and ridicule, and finally died a death infinitely worse than their kind of death. There wasn't much beauty and order about any of it, but it had to be done.

"There's a time for flowers and candlelight, My daughter, and a time for darkness and discomfort and simple obedience to the will of God."

I drank the sweet, sharp juice of the grape, feeling the power of His words and the rough, steep path before my feet.

My grace is sufficient for you, for my power is made perfect in weakness (2 Cor. 12:9).

Prayer Power

Job 42, which tells how Job prayed for his friends, is exciting because it demonstrates that one who is faithful to God has power to intercede for his friends and loved ones. I can't think of anything more encouraging.

James tells us that "the prayer of a righteous man is powerful and effective" (James 5:16).

At a women's retreat I once heard a young pastor's wife tell how an entire brawling congregation was calmed and healed through her desperate prayers, first for the most obvious troublemaker, and then for those less offensive. Out of that experience a great faith was created within her, and the once floundering church has become a place where prayer flourishes and souls are saved.

Now, in my 60s, I am just beginning to realize how dynamic prayer is. Oh, I have prayed all my life, but I realize, looking back, that many times those prayers were ineffective because I hardly dared to hope they would be answered. I have been influenced during recent years by some great prayer warriors. Juanita Kretschmar, who carries the banner of Jesus Christ, with an early-church fervor, right into the teeming streets of New York City. Janet Page, the "prayer lady" of the Pennsylvania Conference. Rob and Jacquie Randall, who demonstrated before my very eyes how prayer and fasting can turn a church around. There are two young men in our church today whose prayers so activate my own faith that I too become a prayer warrior. I have come to know that when a few individuals band together to pray in faith, change takes place. God is waiting for us to take His promises seriously. To claim them. To storm heaven with them. To expect results.

John gives us another wonderful assurance. "If anyone sees his brother commit a sin that does not lead to death, he should pray and God will give him [the brother] life" (1 John 5:16).

Somehow, we just don't grasp the magnitude of these promises.

Claim that life of which John speaks for those friends, loved ones, and fellow church members whom you see floundering in the battle with sin. Take God at His word. Thank Him for the blessing even as you rise from your knees. I am convinced our prayers often free Him to work for individuals, when He could not have done so otherwise. What a shame if we fail to be faithful intercessors!

As you kneel in prayer today, lift up a friend who's bent beneath pain or sin, fully expecting God to intervene. As He did with Job, He will accept your prayer and deal kindly with the one you love.

After the Lord had said these things to Job, he said to Eliphaz the Temanite, "I am angry with you and your two friends, because you have not spoken of me what is right, as my servant Job has. . . . *My servant Job will pray for you, and I will accept his prayer and not deal with you according to your folly. . . . And the Lord accepted Job's prayer* (Job 42:7-9).

May I Call You Sister?

Our son was 2,000 miles from home. He had little on which to operate except optimism.

He would find work. He would find an inexpensive room. He would not be lonely. He could live on very simple food.

I was trying to believe it all as I went about my work. Trying to imagine him being welcomed in a neat, old-fashioned rooming house by a plump, motherly lady who wouldn't charge him a penny until he received his first paycheck and who fed him wonderful meals because he was a pleasant and courteous young man.

However, I knew life wasn't really like that, so my heart was heavy as I cleaned and cooked for my husband and less adventuresome sons and daughters. (As it turned out, when he was hitchhiking, some men in a pickup stopped and told him to toss his suitcase in the back and hop in. Before he could comply, they roared off with his luggage, leaving him standing by the highway with only the clothes on his back. That's how life really is, but I'm getting off course.)

He knew, our son, that he was on my heart and in my prayers all during his wanderings, and he chuckled at my frettings. Yet I'm sure that if he had any frightened or lonely moments, he was comforted by my concern, for we all need to know that someone cares, whether it be mother, wife, husband, or child.

Did you ever think what life would be like if there were no family unit? If male and female mated and parted, the mother abandoning the young as soon as they could fend for themselves?

Once in a while, at our house, when we're all together, we linger about the dinner table, and the conversation goes back to the days when the children were growing up (they're all adults now). It goes something like this: "Remember the time Mom rode Mitch's Sting Ray around the go-cart track and forgot it had hand brakes?" (Fortunately, the inglorious ending is always drowned in guffaws.)

Other "remembers" fly thick and fast, and there is much laughter. The stories we chuckle over wouldn't be very funny to anyone else, but they are to us because we lived them together. It's important to have someone with whom to recall the yesterdays. That's another thing family is all about.

It isn't considered "cool" today to show much emotion. If it weren't for those blessed people at home who know us so well that it's useless to feign sophistication, we'd have to hide our rejoicing and despair. But within the walls of home a teenager can still dance a little jig over a letter from a certain special someone; a child can shed tears over the bully who harasses him at school; Mom can shyly announce she's been elected president of the PTA, then bask in her family's pleased surprise; and even Dad can admit he's out of sorts because he played lousy golf in a very important game with business friends.

Sometimes it may seem a bit much, all this togetherness under the same roof. Tempers flare, personalities clash. The monastic life beckons. But as one who grew up in an unconventional home situation, let me assure you that there is no loneliness quite like the lack of family. Although food, clothing, and even love are provided, there is something within that does not wish the generations disturbed. We need a father and mother, however imperfect. We need brothers and sisters, however unlike us. And when deprived of family, especially at the roots, we ever wander through life with a sense of loss, searching for something, we know not what.

For those of you who identify all too well with what I'm trying to say, let me add that I have, at last, found my place in the family setup, not just as the wife of a good husband and mother of six, but as a daughter as well. I've even acquired, at long last, a Brother. I've traced my lineage back to my Father, God, and discovered my Brother, Jesus Christ. This Brother loved me so much He came searching for me on a dangerous mission in which He lost His life, but not before He made sure all was well with me. I understand He's your Brother too. I guess that makes us related, doesn't it? See you at the family reunion!

We know that we are children of God (1 John 5:19).

On Plants and People

This morning when I went to get the mail, I treated myself to a little walk up the road. I have to admit it wasn't just for exercise. There's a certain point in the long upgrade where the view of our huge perennial garden is especially lovely. I enjoy it as much as the passers-by do. This particular morning in August all the daylilies are in full bloom, and the pale yellow Hyperions against lavender-blue perovskia are breathtaking. A broad expanse of lawn between the road and the garden is an emerald setting for the riot of color. I marvel at what God and Sylvia have done. For me, it has been a busy summer, too busy, with very little time to dig in the dirt. That's a frustrating state of affairs, but my work for the Lord has first priority.

At any rate, the moment of viewing was rewarding, and I began to plan for the fall planting season as I strolled a bit farther up the hill.

Suddenly I realized the unmown roadside was also ablaze with color. Some would say the wildflowers were at their peak; others would say the weeds were in bloom. It's all in how you look at it, I guess, but weeds or wildflowers, they had a beauty of their own, there in the morning sun. Chicory, blue as the sky; lacy parasols of Queen Anne's lace; fuzzy purple asters; and cheery black-eyed Susans.

But pretty as they were, they remained poor country cousins of the blooms in the cultivated border. Yet my honest gardener's heart knew that every plant in the perennial border had started out as a weed or wildflower. What had made the difference? How had the humble swamp flag become an elegant iris? The bold invasive field yarrow the soft tapestry-like pastel achillea? And also, the carefully planned design of the border put the roadside to shame. A lot of factors had determined the difference between the two.

Thousands of botanists in many lands and throughout hundreds of years have worked patiently, lovingly, painstakingly to bring about the array of blooms available in gardening catalogs today. From the housewife who plants a few marigolds and petunias around her birdbath to the horticulturist who cares for Butchart Gardens (don't ever live out your life without seeing Butchart Gardens!), we all benefit from their scientific discoveries.

Though I am only a beginner, having gained my meager horticultural education from extensive reading, I understand that once the botanist and horticulturist have completed their work, I must know how to prepare the soil and arrange plants attractively. The purple-pale yellow-silver color scheme that I chose, necessitates long hours of studying bloom time, height, location (sun or shade?), zone (will it survive the winter here in zone 5?), soil (wet or dry, light or heavy?) for each plant. Small wonder that the cultivated border outshines the scraggly roadside weeds. It took a lot of us to bring about that result.

It occurred to me this morning that we all start out like the roadside tangle. But God sees in each of us the potential for a glorious garden. If we but lend ourselves to the process, He will begin a most miraculous work in us through the Holy Spirit. A work of hybridizing, if you will, nurturing the finer qualities of our character and removing the negative traits, until at last we stand in full beauty, reflecting the character of the lovely Jesus.

Just as in the garden, the need for care never stops. Always the plant and the Christian must be nurtured, guarded, rescued from outside forces, and handled gently. Praise God that the heavenly Gardener counts each of us a choice plant, a rare hybrid, a potential specimen for His garden! He does not begrudge the care.

"He [Christ] knows those whose hearts He can fill with the holy oil, that they may impart it to others. Those who faithfully carry forward the work of Christ in our world, representing in word and works the character of God, fulfilling the Lord's purpose for them, are in His sight very precious. Christ takes pleasure in them as a man takes pleasure in a well-kept garden and the fragrance of the flowers he has planted" (*God's Amazing Grace*, p. 95).

Now to him who is able to do immeasurably more than all we ask or imagine, according to his power that is at work within us, to him be glory (Eph. 3:20, 21).

Walking With Friends

I met Verna in fourth grade. We both attended the same two-room school in Vermont. She had moved to Wolcott that year from a nearby town, and I can't remember how we broke the shyness barrier, but it was instant friendship, a friendship that never wavered until life propelled us far apart and into different worlds. Even today we keep in touch.

She lived right in the village, only moments from the schoolhouse. I, not so fortunate, walked two miles back and forth to the halls of learning. Many nights after school she'd walk me along the dusty road to the bend from which I could see our farmhouse. We'd sit on a rock in the sunshine and chat awhile; then it was not uncommon for me to walk back a ways with her before turning homeward once more. Our parents questioned our sanity. All that useless walking. But we loved every minute of it. We had so many things to say to each other, so many silly secrets to share, so many dreams to exchange.

When at last we parted, we'd turn and wave until the bend in the road blocked our view. Those hours with a special person made my school days a warm and happy experience, and remembering them even now makes me smile.

Later in my life there was another series of walks that were critical to my entire future. While I attended Atlantic Union College I worked in the book bindery each afternoon. I always filled out my time card at the close of the day with a happy heart, for I knew the young man who is now my husband (and no longer young) would be waiting at the door to walk me to the girls' dorm. It was often nearly dark and bitter cold. The distance between the two buildings was far too short, and each moment was precious. There could be no dallying, for propriety was the order of the day, but we managed a hasty, half-frozen kiss now and then. We've walked a good many lovely places since, but probably none were sweeter than those campus strolls in the mid-1940s. They marked the point at which our lives came together, simply, naturally, without question or doubt, as though our previous 17 years had been but a prelude to that moment.

There have been other walks that linger in the memory like a fragrance. During heavy New England snowstorms, my academy roommate and I sometimes rose at daybreak and trudged around the campus in the knee-deep snow, reveling in the downfall that nearly obliterated our vision. We liked being the first to leave a path in the unbroken expanse of white. Those memories are rich with youth and laughter.

There was not an endless array of activities in those days, and it was not unusual to go walking with a friend. In fact, sometimes it still isn't. A father told me recently that he and his daughter are going to hike around Prince Edward Island together. Now, that's my idea of an adventure, and one the two will cherish forever.

I don't know about you, but I've been walking with God for many years. I wish I could say it has always been joyful. The truth is, I've not been a consistently pleasant partner. Sometimes my sinful nature leads me stubbornly along a different path than the one He chooses, and I wander far from Him and feel very hopeless. It takes so long to catch up. When I do, He's always glad to see me and never admonishes me, but even so, I know it's very dangerous to be away from Him . . . and very lonely. My greatest desire is to find the perfect rhythm in our journeying, to match my steps to His, to find at the end of the road that I have become like Him, fit to enter His home. It's my prayer for you, too.

I guide you in the way of wisdom and lead you along straight paths. When you walk, your steps will not be hampered; when you run, you will not stumble (Prov. 4:11, 12).

Celebrating Birth

I am sitting alone in our son's darkened living room . . . waiting. A porch light illumines softly, and now and then a car goes by. I have tried to sleep, but it's not a time for sleeping. I am waiting for a baby to be born and am pacing mentally outside the hospital birthing room, while in reality I baby-sit the sleeping firstborn upstairs.

They left for the hospital, our son and his wife, about an hour and a half ago. Her contractions were strong and close together then. Surely it should be all over now. I try not to think of the things that could go wrong. I cannot bear for this sunny, sweet girl, who is so dear to me, to suffer.

I pray for her. That is all I can do.

It takes time to have a baby. I know that. But to my heart it seems to be taking far too much time.

I remind God what a special girl she is. Of all her kindness, her faithfulness to Him.

Midnight.

1:00 a.m.

1:30 a.m. Headlights rounding the corner into the driveway. Mitch coming up the back steps, through the kitchen and into the semi-lit living room. An eagerness, born of relief and joy, in his step, in his voice.

It's a girl! (Just what we'd all wanted to complement the 2-year-old boy sleeping upstairs.)

A quick, uncomplicated delivery. (Thank You, Lord.)

Mother doing fine. Announced she was hungry.

Baby active and healthy.

A girl! I can't believe it.

We are both too high to sleep, so chat for a bit, not caring that it's the middle of the night and that the morrow will be busy. I think to myself it has to be one of life's best moments, to share with a cherished son one of the mountaintop experiences of his life.

After 6,000 years the birth of a new life upon our battered old planet is still cause for celebration. What a gift God gave in our ability to create little people who knit together the bloodlines of two separate families.

Even God Himself became involved, letting His own Son slip through the gates of heaven to be joined with the family of earth, knitting together the universal community with the lost planet.

When the Bethlehem Babe made His humble entrance into this world, it was at great risk, for into the pure heavenly bloodline came the weakness and deterioration of marred humanity.

But, praise God, it did not contaminate or overcome. Because Jesus clung to His Divine Father, aware of His need, aware of His danger, He is able to offer us, today, a life beyond our pitiful heritage, and eventually a holy eternity in which the sins of the fathers no longer visit the children. In which one does not look into the face of a newborn and wonder what evil traits we have bequeathed him or her.

Jesus truly is the Light of the world. How dark and hopeless would be our outlook if He had not become the breakthrough in human history. Mary's labor that night in the stable resulted in the birth of all births. Our release from captivity. A bright candle illuminating gross darkness. No wonder the angels sang!

Every time we bring a wee one home from the hospital, our hearts should rejoice for that Babe in swaddling clothes, destined for rejection, sorrow, and death that our little ones might have hope.

I, a grandmother for the seventh time, lift Him up to you as Saviour and King not only of our brand-new Allison June, but also of your children and grandchildren, whoever and wherever they are. Give Him praise. Give Him honor. Give Him gratitude.

For to us a child is born, to us a son is given (Isa. 9:6).

Storm Warnings

Tonight the long arms of the Norway spruces are flinging themselves about as if in some woeful torment, and thickly falling snow swirls in clouds around our big red barn. The driveway has disappeared into unfamiliar drifts mounding high on every side. We are in the midst of the "blizzard of '93" or the "storm of the century" as the media have grandly entitled it.

Yesterday morning Don and I left Sanibel Island, Florida, where we had been vacationing for two weeks. Sadly we walked to the beach for the last time to watch the peaceful aqua surf tumble lazily against the sand. We scuffed among the shells, searching for the last coquina, and stood for a moment observing a huge pileated woodpecker persistently whacking a hole into a defenseless palm. I marveled again at the tree's silky fronds glistening against the perfect blue of the sky. I'm not really a tropical person, nor one who minds snow over-much, but I had to admit that those sun-drenched weeks had had about them a touch of paradise.

Reluctantly we tossed our luggage into the trunk of our rental car and headed for the Ft. Myers Airport, stopping along the way at our favorite fruit stand to pick up bags of grapefruit.

Coming in over LaGuardia Airport we noted that there was little snow. Later as we landed in Rochester, our destination, we noted again that there was no great accumulation and that the highways were bare. The sun was even shining. "I told you it would be almost spring when we got home," I said smugly to Don, my mind already dancing with visions of crocus abloom and tulips breaking through the chilly sod.

But moments later our daughter, Amy, who met us at the airport, pricked my spring balloon. "We need to stop at Wegman's so you can get groceries. A blizzard is predicted for tomorrow, and who knows how long we'll be housebound, so you'd better stock up."

I was not in the mood for shopping. I just wanted to get home. "Maybe we could pick up a gallon of milk somewhere," I said. "You know how excited those weather forecasters get over every little storm system."

"Mom, be serious. We're supposed to get 50-mile-an-hour winds, and you know what that's like when it's snowing. You have very little food in your house."

I looked at the huge red ball sinking slowly into the horizon, that old ditty "Red at night, sailor's delight" sing-songing in my mind, and tried to internalize her dire warnings. I just couldn't switch from tropical euphoria to this state-of-emergency mind-set. Don, however, who has a healthy appetite, didn't waver. "We'll stop at Wegman's," he decided. "Blizzard or no blizzard, we need some food on the shelves."

Outvoted, I entered the store, filled the cart with all the proper things, and we drove home in the last rays of sunlight.

And sure enough, here we are 24 hours later in a blizzard. The radio spits out the old familiar warnings. All roads officially closed. No traffic allowed. Do not leave your home.

I'm thankful Amy and Don dragged me to the store. Thankful we have a generator in case we lose electrical power. Thankful we have a sturdy snow-blower for our driveway. Thankful we own a four-wheel drive vehicle. Thankful we are prepared!

I expect that before Noah's flood the people had tropical euphoria. They, too, could not shift into a state-of-emergency mind-set. But the Flood came, and only those who were prepared lived through it.

Another cry now rings across our planet. "Blow the trumpet in Zion; sound the alarm on my holy hill. Let all who live in the land tremble, for the day of the Lord is coming. It is close at hand" (Joel 2:1). An event far more profound than flood or blizzard lies before us. It's tempting to coast with the familiar, to ignore preparation, to shelter one's mind from worrisome thoughts, but this upcoming event demands change, sober dedication, diligent prayer.

Only those who sort reality from fantasy will move on to a genuine paradise. Those who see the present as too sweet to abandon will have made a costly choice. Don't get trapped in tropical euphoria. A true storm lies ahead.

The Lord will roar from Zion and thunder from Jerusalem; the earth and sky will tremble. But the Lord will be a refuge for his people" (Joel 2:16).

Daily Devotionals for *Women*

•

Among Friends

This daily devotional draws together the wisdom and creativity of more than 150 Adventist women from around the world. Representing all walks of life, they open their hearts, sharing thoughts, feelings, and ideas about things that matter most to them. They speak candidly about their problems and worries. They rejoice at evidences of God's love. Join this celebration of friendship among women who love the Lord and enjoy the spiritual refreshment and fellowship these devotionals bring. Rose Otis, editor. Hardcover with dust jacket, 432 pages. US$14.95, Cdn$18.70.

•

The Listening Heart

If God's voice sometimes seems silent, hushed by the busyness of your life, take a few moments each day to contemplate His love as demonstrated in the lives of other women like you. Writing from around the world, they share how He has sustained them through doubt, brought gentle healing, opened unexpected doors, and filled their lives with purpose and joy. Day by day their experiences will bring you an ever deepening sense of God's presence. Rose Otis, editor. Hardcover with dust jacket. US$14.95, Cdn$18.70. A matching journal is available.

•

To order, call **1-800-765-6955** or write to ABC Mailing Service, P.O. Box 1119, Hagerstown, MD 21741. Send check or money order. Enclose applicable sales tax and 15 percent (minimum US$2.50) for postage and handling. Prices and availability subject to change without notice. Add GST in Canada.